For the first time in history, this star-studded book profiles 20 of the greatest soccer legends drawn from both sides of the Irish border.

Written as an accompaniment to the RTÉ Radio 1 series *Ireland's Soccer Top 20*, the book traces the sport's evolution in Ireland from the late 1930s to the present day.

Among those featured are some of football's greatest names – Johnny Giles, Roy Keane, George Best, Paul McGrath, Pat Jennings, Liam Brady, Derek Dougan, David O'Leary, Ronnie Whelan, Don Givens and Frank Stapleton.

Memories of the Republic of Ireland's historic matches in the 1930s, '40s and '50s are featured in chapters on Manchester United's Jackie Carey and Aston Villa's Con Martin.

Former Manchester United players Noel Cantwell and Tony Dunne along with Preston North End's Alan Kelly reminisce about the 1960s. Norman Whiteside, Packie Bonner, Niall Quinn and Damien Duff recall more recent times.

Ireland's Soccer Top 20 encompasses some of football's greatest moments, among them FA Cup and Championship successes, European triumphs and wonderful international campaigns including Euro '88 and six World Cups. This 'Hall of Fame' of Irish soccer is required reading for all football fans.

For Seán

IRELAND'S
SOCCER
TOP
20

Colm Keane

MAINSTREAM
PUBLISHING
EDINBURGH AND LONDON

First published in Great Britain in 2004 by
MAINSTREAM PUBLISHING (EDINBURGH) LTD
7 Albany Street
Edinburgh EH1 3UG

ISBN 1 84018 578 3

A catalogue record for this book is available from the British Library

Typeset in Berkeley and Gill Sans Condensed

Printed in Great Britain by
Mackays of Chatham plc

CONTENTS

INTRODUCTION

WHEN GEORGE BEST LEFT BELFAST FOR MANCHESTER UNITED IN 1961, HE WAS ONLY 15. He travelled by boat to Liverpool and on by train to Manchester, understandably overcome by apprehension at the prospect of what lay ahead. Not surprisingly, he and his young companion got lost, ending up some distance away from their final destination. When he eventually arrived, he entered a world of boarding-houses, landladies, homesickness and tearful nights. Like any lost child, he quickly returned home.

In retrospect, the Irish soccer trade with Britain was a cruel business. Young Irish players took boats and trains to cities like London, Manchester, Liverpool and Birmingham in search of success. Separated from family and friends, many struggled to survive. Most packed it in. Others were rejected, having failed to impress. More dropped down to lower divisions, where they carved out modest careers. It was, in many respects, callous exploitation, with fragile youngsters subject to the whims of their bosses and discarded at will.

Ever since the advent of professional soccer in England in the late 1800s, talented Irish footballers moved cross-channel. The big clubs – many of them founder members of the Football League in 1888 – picked the cream of the crop. By the early 1900s, stars from Northern Ireland were winning FA Cup medals with Everton, Spurs and Newcastle United. In the Irish Free State's first home international in 1927, players from Aston Villa, Derby County, Leeds United and Everton lined out against Italy. Football's free market was already in action.

Attracted by the promise of a wage, the talent continued to move. In the early 1900s, scouts toured Ireland, north and south, offering pay-packets of £4 a week. With the burgeoning working class cramming stadiums, the pay was derisory. This was particularly true in the wealthy heartland of industrial Britain. For club owners, it was cheap labour. For players, it was an improvement on comparable rates in industry, the shipyards, the railways or down mines. There were, however, no bulging bank accounts. Once a player's career came to a close, bare survival normally followed.

In the mid-1940s, the emigrant trail took off with a vengeance. Spurred on by a massive rise in public interest, post-war football boomed in England. Crowds flocked to matches. Turnstiles clicked furiously as attendance records were broken year after year. In the 1949–50 season over 40 million people paid to watch soccer. Inevitably, huge stars emerged. Among them, from both sides of the Irish border, were Jackie Carey, Peter Farrell, Tommy Eglington, Con Martin, Danny Blanchflower, Jimmy McIlroy and Billy Bingham. These were exceptional players, all signed at low cost from across the Irish Sea.

By the time the maximum wage was abolished in 1961, the export trade was thriving. Fuelled even further by England's World Cup success in 1966 and helped by the spread of TV, professional football entered a new era. Irish players like George Best and Tony Dunne, who were part of the European Cup-winning Manchester United side of 1968, became internationally famous. Johnny Giles went on to enormous acclaim with Leeds United, having begun his career at Old Trafford. Goalkeepers like Pat Jennings and Alan Kelly, and players like Noel Cantwell and Derek Dougan, all made their mark. The era of Irish-born star footballers had arrived.

Throughout the 1970s and '80s, the exploitation intensified. Old box cameras captured fresh-faced teenagers like Liam Brady, Frank Stapleton and David O'Leary setting out on their journeys. Commuters at Belfast Airport were joined by schoolboy Norman Whiteside on his way to play for the Manchester United juniors. This was Irish soccer at its peak, feeding an extraordinary exodus of Irish youngsters to hungry soccer clubs in all parts of Britain.

They were paid poor wages. For many, their days were badly structured, tempting them to frequent pool-halls and gaming arcades. Promises of a school education fell by the wayside. The threat of injury was ever-present. The danger of managerial changes or club clear-outs overshadowed their careers. Luckily, some had relatives to stay with or friends to share worries with. No matter, images of emotional departures, lonely bedrooms and sleepless nights still dominated their lives.

That so many emerged unscathed, performing with top clubs, was remarkable. Brady, Stapleton and O'Leary went on to huge success at Arsenal, with Brady also starring for Juventus and Stapleton playing for Manchester United. Like Brady, Don Givens made his mark on the Continent, attaining legendary status at Neuchâtel Xamax. Ronnie Whelan made the smooth transition from Home Farm to Liverpool, where he shared in six League titles and a European Cup triumph with one of the finest sides in British football history. Inevitably, quality players like these also prompted international success, bringing a new credibility to Ireland's standing in world football.

How a tiny island could produce two international teams that would reach six World Cup finals is hard to fathom. But that's exactly what happened. Derek Dougan was part of Northern Ireland's historic adventure at the 1958 World Cup finals in Sweden. Pat Jennings and Norman Whiteside, who also feature in this book, played for Northern Ireland in the finals in 1982 and 1986. Players like Packie Bonner and Paul McGrath propelled the Republic of Ireland to the finals in 1990 and 1994. Niall Quinn and Roy Keane made it to one or other of those finals, while Damien Duff won acclaim in Korea and Japan in 2002. Few countries of comparable size could come close to this record.

Inevitably, the players in this book played a central role in shaping and moulding the story of Irish soccer's progress and success. Through their talent and commitment, each played a part. Between them, they won scores of Championships and Cup medals. They played in the world's great stadiums. They outshone and outplayed the finest international stars. While doing so, they displayed a standard of excellence that marked them out from their peers. They also left behind the sort of magical memories only exceptional talents leave in their wake. For those memories alone, their legend is assured.

As always, many people deserve thanks for their help with this book and the accompanying radio series. In particular, I am grateful to Adrian Moynes, Eithne Hand, Tony O'Donoghue and Lorelei Harris, all of RTÉ, for their support. Fionnuala Hayes transcribed the raw interviews with her usual care and dedication. Noel Roberts compiled the programmes with diligence and skill. Credit also to the various RTÉ archives and libraries for their efforts.

Ned Keane from Villierstown, County Waterford, was generous with his time, knowledge and invaluable suggestions. That great broadcaster Philip Greene was always available to steer me in the right direction. Ed Mulhall, Managing Director of News in RTÉ, provided guidance at critical moments. In addition, William 'Nooche' Kenefick and Donal Cullinane, both from County Cork, assisted at the early stages.

I am grateful to Bray Wanderers' manager Pat Devlin who, as agent and advisor to Damien Duff, set up the interview with the Republic of Ireland star. A similar debt is owed to Michael Kennedy, solicitor and agent to Roy Keane, who was a pleasure to deal with. Jackie Ryan from Bray, along with P.J. Gannon and Ray Connor of the Dublin Arsenal Supporters' Club, were full of enthusiasm. Norman, from Inpho, helped with the centre-page photographs and the front cover. Likewise, my appreciation to Bill Campbell, Peter MacKenzie and all the staff at Mainstream Publishing who were, once again, a joy to work with, especially Lizzie, Ailsa, Elaine, Graeme, Fiona, Becky, Claire and Sharon, as well as Lorraine McCann.

Many hundreds of players, supporters, commentators and people from all walks of life provided further help and advice. Although too many to mention by name, some I must single out. Michael Kelleher of Bray Public Library identified useful research sources. My son Seán Keane and Úna O'Hagan read the raw chapters and provided lots of encouragement. Without both, the book would never have been completed. Former Manchester United captain and Republic of Ireland legend Noel Cantwell was kindness personified. My thanks also to former international Seamus Dunne, whose insights to Jackie Carey were of inestimable value.

Lastly, I wish to thank all the contributors for telling me their stories and recalling their careers. Some come from long-forgotten eras. Others have more recently retired. A few continue to play. Many lined out side by side. More were deadly adversaries for club and country. But what they all have in common is that mark of greatness, that indefinable quality that sets them apart as outstanding exponents of the game of soccer. To them all, we will always be grateful.

Colm Keane
August 2004

I. CON MARTIN

IT WAS BILLED AS ONE OF THE GREAT MISMATCHES IN THE HISTORY OF FOOTBALL.
England lined out with Billy Wright of Wolves at right-half. They also
had Wilf Mannion of Middlesbrough and Tom Finney of Preston
North End. The great Bert Williams of Wolves was in goal. They had
never before lost on home ground to foreign opposition. They
certainly were unlikely to lose this match, which was being played at
Goodison Park. In sharp contrast, the Republic of Ireland team was
a collection of disparate talents. The wonderful Jackie Carey of
Manchester United was captain. The equally talented Peter Farrell of
Everton and Con Martin of Aston Villa were in the side. But Ireland
had lost seven of their last nine games and had two Shamrock Rovers
players in key positions. Quite simply, they arrived at the match as
no-hopers.

That early autumn day in 1949, over 50,000 spectators were
crammed into Goodison Park. From the kick-off, England all but
assaulted the Republic of Ireland goal. Dozens of attacks were
repelled. Then the unexpected happened. A penalty was awarded to
Ireland. Con Martin slammed the ball to the back of the net. The
score at half-time was 1–0. In the second half, England's onslaught
continued. In the dying minutes came another goal. It was scored by
Peter Farrell. The Irish spectators were ecstatic. The old enemy was
laid low. Old-timers remember it well – the date 21 September 1949,
the score 2–0, the day when history was made and England's historic
home record was shattered.

'We stayed in a hotel at Southport, just outside Liverpool,' Con
Martin, who played centre-half that day, recalls. 'We had a little get-
together and we spoke about the match. As we drove to the match I
got a bit nervous because we were playing against a very good side.

It looked as though we were going to be hammered. But our goalkeeper Tommy Godwin had a wonderful game and the defence held out very well. It suddenly dawned on me in the second half that we had a chance.

'We had great support from the Irish people in Liverpool and there were lots of Irish people who travelled over by boat to see the match. As a matter of fact, there were about 20,000 people representing Ireland on that particular day. I was lucky enough to score a goal from the penalty spot and Peter Farrell eventually scored a goal in the second half to give us a well-deserved victory. It gave us a great result at Goodison Park.

'England were the best team in Europe at the time. Our team really hadn't got a chance. But we had a great game, our defence played very well and lucky enough we came out winners 2–0. One particular columnist said that he'd eat his hat if Ireland beat England. I don't know whether he ever did eat his hat or not. But that was a historic victory and the result was great for us. We were the first foreign team to beat England on home soil. It was a great occasion.'

Recollections of the 1940s are normally bathed in a soft, warm glow. Images of Hovis, Bovril and oatmeal porridge colour our memories. Fans wore flat caps, oversized brown coats and sported lean, hungry faces. They turned up at Dalymount Park hoping for improbable victories over impossibly glamorous teams. Crowds of more than 40,000 crammed into matches. They looked to the game for entertainment and as an escape from hard times. These, after all, were hungry years when football was a part of the fabric of working-class life.

The 1940s was an era featuring huge stars whose magnificent talents lit up the sporting stage. In England players like Stanley Matthews, Tommy Lawton, Stan Mortensen and Wilf Mannion dominated the game. Irish stars included Kevin O'Flanagan, Tommy Eglington and Paddy Coad. But no Irish star surpassed the great Con Martin, who played for Drumcondra, Glentoran, Leeds United and Aston Villa. He was, it's widely agreed, one of Ireland's greatest exports and one of the country's finest football exponents.

'I was stationed in Baldonnel, in the Air Corps, as an apprentice aircraft mechanic,' Con says of the early 1940s. 'We were advised to play games like basketball, tennis, soccer and Gaelic football. I played a lot of Gaelic football for St Mary's of Saggart. I represented Dublin. In fact, I was unlucky, due to "The Ban", that I didn't win an All-Ireland medal. There was a ban at the time that if you played soccer you weren't allowed to play Gaelic.

'There was an officer in Baldonnel whose brother was the secretary of Drumcondra. He saw me play a few times for the Air Corps and invited me to join Drumcondra. I went down for a trial and I was signed and I played with them for about three or four years. It was while I was there that I was invited up to the North of Ireland to play for Glentoran.'

While playing with Glentoran, Con Martin made the first of his 30 international appearances for what was then known as the Irish Free State. That first cap was won in 1946 as a sub against Portugal at the Stadium of Light in Lisbon. Although selected as an outfield player, Con replaced the injured Ned Courtney in goal after 30 minutes. Drawing on his knowledge of Gaelic football, he readily took to his unfamiliar role and kept a clean sheet for the rest of the match. Selected in nets for the game against Spain in Madrid a week later, he again kept a clean sheet while shining in the Free State's historic 1–0 victory. Remarkably, the international career of Ireland's great outfield player had begun with two spectacular performances in nets.

'I played for Ireland as a goalkeeper in Portugal and Spain and I had a very good game in 1946 against the Spanish,' Con recollects. 'I had been drafted in as a goalkeeper after Ned Courtney had cried off and they had nobody else to put in. I had a great game to such an extent that the Spanish forwards couldn't score a goal and we were fortunate enough to come out winners. I remember in the audience that day was General Franco. I was lucky enough to shake his hand at the end of the match. That was my fondest memory of playing football for Ireland.

'As a matter of fact, I was the only goalkeeper for Ireland who never had a goal scored against him. As a result, I was recommended by Jackie Carey to go to Manchester United as a goalkeeper. Matt Busby came up to Belfast and wanted to sign me but I preferred to go to Leeds as a centre-half because I felt that I would be better represented as a centre-half rather than as a goalkeeper. I fancied outfield rather than playing in goal. Eventually they sold me to Leeds.'

Con Martin arrived at Leeds United just in time for one of the club's most disastrous eras. Not long after he signed, they sank from the First Division with an appallingly low 18 points from 42 games to show for their season's efforts. That relegation in 1947 inevitably sealed Con's departure and he was soon on his way to Aston Villa. There he settled into a team that consistently held its own in the First Division. Villa were genuine contenders for football supremacy alongside Arsenal, Wolves, Manchester United, Newcastle and Portsmouth.

'Aston Villa were a very good club,' Con says. 'They had players like Danny Blanchflower and Davy Walsh. They were great players. Another player there, who at a different stage played with Preston North End, was Tommy Thompson. The crowds were fantastic. I remember playing a Cup match in Villa Park and there were 75,000 people there. We had a great result and we went on further in the Cup. I was originally a centre-half but being connected with Gaelic football I was able to catch the ball and I represented Aston Villa as a goalkeeper and full-back and centre-half and on one occasion I was in at centre-forward.

'It was just after the war and things weren't too bright in England. Things weren't too good with regard even to food. It was very scarce and we were lucky enough that people used to send us parcels of food from Ireland. There was a lot of Irish in Birmingham at the time and we managed pretty well. Our pay wasn't all that great. The crowds were so big that you'd imagine we'd get more. But we only got about £14 a week, which was a lot of money then, and we got £20 for playing international football.

'In those days the leather ball was very prominent and it was difficult to kick it a distance. Nowadays they have a plastic ball and it's a lot easier to play than it was in our day. But I was with a great club and they looked after us very well. There were lots of Irish people there and we became very friendly with them. Aston Villa were very good to me and even to this day they invite me over to see a match once every season.'

Up to the start of the 1950s, demarcation lines between soccer north and south of the border had yet to be properly defined. Back in the early days it wasn't uncommon for players from both jurisdictions to turn out for each other's teams. Inevitably, a player of

Con's calibre was called on to play for both sides. From his time with Glentoran through Leeds United right up to his early years with Aston Villa, Con Martin was a dual international.

'In those days you could play for the North of Ireland and you could play for the South of Ireland,' Con recalls. 'Some of the Northern Ireland players played with us, and vice versa. I first represented the North of Ireland in Hampden Park against Scotland. I was a travelling reserve but one of the players got injured and I was brought into the team. I played in a position that wasn't very familiar to me, at right half-back. We got a great result in Glasgow that day. We drew 0–0 with Scotland. It was a great occasion for me to play for Northern Ireland.

'I represented them on about six occasions but then I refused to play for Northern Ireland any more due to circumstances at Aston Villa. I remember playing for Northern Ireland against Wales in Wrexham. I got a telephone call from the FAI asking me to refuse to play for Northern Ireland. At that late stage I just said I couldn't do it because it was too late. But the same day that Ireland and Wales were playing, Aston Villa were playing Manchester United and Manchester United trounced Aston Villa at Old Trafford. I arrived back at the Villa grounds and the chairman brought me up to his office and asked me, for Aston Villa's sake, to refuse to play for Northern Ireland. So I did it. I refused to play for Northern Ireland from then on, and that was the end of the story.'

Throughout the first half of the 1950s, Con Martin continued to excel for Aston Villa and became a central figure in the club's League and Cup campaigns. Villa remained a major force in English football, coming sixth in both 1951–52 and 1954–55. The club's battles with the greats of the day, including Wolves and Blackpool, were legendary. Arsenal, Tottenham and Chelsea led the challenge from London. From Manchester came a group of young players who were fast being referred to as the Busby Babes. In company like this Con Martin spent his eight seasons at Aston Villa, playing primarily at centre-half but also turning out in many positions, including in goal.

'The Busby Babes were a great team and they had some great players,' Con recalls. 'They were reckoned to be the best team in England at the time. They were all very young players and very fit players and they had a great manager in Matt Busby. Duncan

Edwards was a very powerful young fellow who went on to play international football for England. Bobby Charlton was another. They were a very good side and we always had difficulty playing against them.

'I can remember playing against them one holiday period when we had to go to Old Trafford. We were lucky enough to beat them at Old Trafford. The return match with Manchester United was at Villa Park and we beat them again at Villa Park. The outcome was great and we got full points against the Busby Babes.

'I also remember playing for Aston Villa against Preston North End, at Preston, and I was marking a very famous player by the name of Tom Finney. I was playing in the left-back position. He was a very good player. I had a very good game. The chairman congratulated me and the referee came over and spoke to me and he said: "You had a good game today." After the game I was coming home to Dublin via Liverpool to play a match. We used to play in England on a Saturday and then represent our country on a Sunday at Dalymount Park. I had to travel from Preston to Liverpool and from Liverpool to Dublin, arriving at six o'clock in the morning to meet the international team at the Gresham Hotel at 12 o'clock and then play a match in the afternoon against one of those Continental countries. After our great result against Preston our chairman was very pleased and was very helpful in getting me back. He advised me to get a taxi, brought me to Liverpool and came over with me on the boat from Liverpool.

'I had a great relationship with some of the England players. Stanley Matthews was a great player, a very cautious player and a gentleman. I played against him on several occasions. On another occasion, England came to Dalymount Park and I was playing centre-half and I was marking Tommy Lawton and he was a great centre-forward. I was lucky enough to have a good game against him as well.

'Stan Mortensen played for Blackpool. He was a fiery sort of fellow and a great goal-scorer. He was a great player. He played centre-forward for Blackpool and he also played with England. He played in the Cup final and he scored a brilliant goal. I can always remember his company; he was a very nice chap to know. Stanley Matthews and Stan Mortensen became very friendly with me. We used to go to

Blackpool for a holiday period and we'd meet them there. We enjoyed their company. I can remember Stanley Matthews coming up to us and saying how bad we were as a football team at Aston Villa.'

On the international front, since 1950 Con Martin was available only to the Republic of Ireland and had given up appearing with the North. From then on, he was an automatic choice in the Republic's team, playing mainly at the heart of defence and slotting in alongside footballers like Alf Ringstead of Sheffield United, Arthur Fitzsimons of Middlesbrough, Jackie Carey of Manchester United, Tommy Eglington of Everton and Frank O'Farrell of West Ham United. Since the Republic of Ireland Act, which came into effect in 1949, the country had formally changed its name and political status. Unfortunately, that didn't stop the team from falling to heavy defeats against Spain, Austria, West Germany and France, although they did beat Austria, Norway, Holland and Luxembourg, and chalked up one major victory against West Germany.

'The international matches were played on the Sunday,' Con says. 'We had to represent our club on the Saturday and travel over after playing our game with Aston Villa. It was very difficult; it's much easier now to play. But the crowds at Dalymount Park were absolutely fantastic. There would be in or around 40,000 or 50,000 there and they were wonderful. We managed all right and we had great times together. There were friendly relationships between the players and with the managers and the Football Association of Ireland.

'We had a fairly good side in the South of Ireland. We had players like Peter Farrell, Tommy Eglington and Davy Walsh. They were class players in the First Division in England at the time. I played in several positions. I played at centre-half, which I preferred. But there were times when I played in goal and I played left-back and right-back. I represented Ireland in about six different positions and on one occasion, when Brendan Carroll had to go off as centre-forward, I was asked to play in the centre-forward position. It was a game against Finland, where we beat them 3–0 and I was lucky enough to score two goals.'

In 1956 Con Martin played his last game for the Republic of Ireland in a 4–1 away victory over Holland. In that game a new generation of players was coming on stream, including Noel Cantwell of West Ham United, Liam Whelan of Manchester United and Joe Haverty of Arsenal. Within a year the side would narrowly miss out on qualification for the 1958 World Cup finals in Sweden. However, they would do so without the inspirational Con Martin leading them on. Although Con's son Mick Martin would later keep the family name alive while playing for Manchester United, West Bromwich Albion, Newcastle United and the Republic of Ireland, the great man himself was beginning to fade. In fact, in 1956 he quit both Aston Villa and the Republic of Ireland, bringing to a close one of the finest careers in the history of Irish football.

'In those days, when you were beginning to get on a bit in years as a professional footballer, when you were over 30, you were on the way out,' Con concludes. 'I lasted until I was about 33 years of age and was invited home to play for Waterford. So I packed in Aston Villa and came home and played for Waterford and that was the end of it. But I'd had a great career. I had 20 years playing as a professional footballer and as a sportsman, and I enjoyed every minute of it.

'I had a wonderful career not alone in soccer but in Gaelic football as well. I have very fond memories of all those players I played against and with, players like Stan Mortensen and Stanley Matthews and Tom Finney. I enjoyed my time as a professional footballer and most of all I enjoyed my time with Aston Villa, where I played for about eight years. I have very fond memories of my stay in Birmingham with Aston Villa. I won a lot of trophies and a lot of medals, which I have put away safely. I look back on it with fond memories and I was very happy with my career as a footballer.'

2. JACKIE CAREY

IT'S HARDLY SURPRISING THAT JACKIE CAREY WAS VOTED FOOTBALLER OF THE YEAR IN 1949. As captain of Manchester United he had led his team through one of the brightest eras in the club's history. His United side hadn't won the League title yet – that would have to wait until 1952. Yet they had won the FA Cup in 1948, had come second in the League for three consecutive years and had a skipper who was rated as one of the finest to wear the captain's armband. What's more, Jackie was about to lead the Republic of Ireland to a historic victory over England at Goodison Park in September 1949.

By all accounts, Jackie Carey was one of the finest footballers and captains ever to play soccer. An avuncular, laid-back pipe smoker, he exhibited a cool, calm demeanour both on and off the field of play. The perfect leader, his confidence and authority were an inspiration to colleagues who looked to him for guidance and advice. Fellow players talk of his quiet words of wisdom, his kindness and his support in times of personal or professional crisis. Whatever their connection with Jackie, no one has anything but the kindest words to say of the man. Indeed, the word 'gentleman' seems to have been specially devised to describe Jackie Carey.

The skills he displayed with Manchester United from the late 1930s to the early 1950s were immaculate. He had a wonderful sense of pace, timing and precision-passing. People refer to his simple style. He delivered beautiful balls. He enjoyed nothing better than sweet movements and graceful build-ups from defence to attack. He loved playing football. No wonder Matt Busby saw him as the quintessential leader and captain. In fact, the fusion that brought together Manchester United, Matt Busby and the concept of fluid, free-flowing football first found expression within a decade of the young 17-year-old Dubliner's arrival at Old Trafford. Spotted playing in Dublin by Manchester United's legendary scout Louis Rocca, Jackie Carey made the short trip cross-channel in 1936.

'I remember him from the start,' Philip Greene, the eminent Radio Éireann commentator, recalls. 'He was just another name, another player then. He played with Home Farm and was an amateur with them. He was a smashing youth player and all eyes were on him. He was then transferred to St James's Gate, which surprised a lot of people. But he only lasted a short time there. United had their eye on him. I don't think that anybody who saw him play even then was surprised that he was signed by United.'

From his first appearance with Manchester United in 1937, Jackie Carey caught the eye. At that time the club were stuck in the Second Division. The stay was short-lived, however, as in his first season they won promotion as runners-up to Aston Villa. Back in the top-flight again, the future looked rosy and promising. Sadly, few could have predicted the impact that the forthcoming war would have on soccer in Britain. It also would rob Jackie Carey of a large chunk of his life as a footballer.

Having enlisted in the British Army, Jackie was eventually shipped to Italy. While there he again took to football, appearing with a number of teams and acquiring the nickname 'Cario'. On returning to Britain he slotted back into the Manchester United side, where his name was soon on the tips of everyone's tongues. Known as Johnny Carey – the 'Jackie' of Dublin and Ireland being replaced by the 'Johnny' more commonly used in England – he soon became a national star. Alongside players like Crompton, Aston, Pearson, Chilton, Rowley and Mitten, Jackie Carey produced some of the finest football of his career. The result was three second-place finishes in the First Division from 1947 to 1949.

'He played the game in a style that Manchester United used, which was simple passing,' Noel Cantwell, the Republic of Ireland international who later took over as captain at United, says. 'He was a good link player. I saw him play at Highbury when I went to West Ham and I went over to see Arsenal play Man United. He played in midfield there and everything he did was simple. It was a bit like the way Roy Keane plays. He was good at passing and supporting, good at angles, a good tackler and of course he was big enough and tall enough to be very good in the air. He had a great all-round ability. He was also one of those guys who never got flustered. He just took things in his stride. That was Johnny Carey.'

In 1948 Jackie Carey had the honour of leading his Manchester United team-mates up the steps at Wembley Stadium to collect the FA Cup. The trophy presentation followed a cracking game against a Blackpool side containing Stanley Matthews and Stan Mortensen. At half-time Carey cautioned his players not to panic. Wise words they proved to be as Blackpool led 2–1 with 20 minutes to go. However, three late goals secured a 4–2 victory that Manchester United so desperately craved. It was to be the high point of United's football story in the 1940s.

More near-misses in the League in 1950 and 1951 were followed by a League Championship triumph in 1952. Although hard to believe, it was Manchester United's first League title in 41 years. Carey captained the side. In a team packed with players of character like Jack Rowley and Stan Pearson, none stood out more prominently than their multi-talented skipper Jackie Carey. To observers it seemed that his mark was to be found literally everywhere in Manchester United's League and Cup campaigns.

'He played everywhere,' Philip Greene recollects. 'He had one distinction that was unbelievable. He played in almost every position for United not just in an emergency during a match but by actually being selected. He was selected in 10 positions. People always think that he wasn't picked in goal but he was actually selected in goal. The one position he was never selected in was outside-left. And that's an almost unbelievable record.

'You couldn't find fault with him as a player. He never fouled. He was always in control. The ball seemed to come to him. He seemed to have some sensitivity about drawing it to him. He had a real football brain. As a player he was absolute perfection. We talk today about Johnny Giles or whoever but there's no player that I ever knew who commanded the game as he commanded it with such poise and excellence. Matt Busby was no fool and the fact that he selected him to play in so many positions says it all.'

As far back as November 1937 Jackie Carey began his long and distinguished career at international level, making his first appearance for the Irish Free State in a 3–3 home draw with Norway.

It's a credit to the player that in 1953, almost 16 years later, he was still playing for the national side, which was then known as the Republic of Ireland. In the interim he displayed the same calm disposition and wonderful skills that he was known for at Manchester United. Unfortunately, internationals were cancelled throughout the war with the result that for seven years Jackie was denied the opportunity to demonstrate his abilities at the highest level. However, shortly after the war concluded he returned to international duty and was soon elevated to the role of team captain.

Those were interesting years at international level. Prior to the war Jackie travelled with the Irish team that drew with both Hungary in Budapest and Germany in Bremen. With the games played within a week of each other in May 1939, the Irish players found themselves in the feverish heat of pre-war Europe. Nazi salutes and pre-match outpourings of National Socialist rhetoric were the order of the day in Bremen. Even in Hungary the presence of a distinguished German government official required the Irish players to raise their arms in salute – something Carey resolutely refused to comply with.

As team captain, he also led his side to that famous 2–0 victory over England at Goodison Park in 1949. Carey's team-talk fired the Irish and inspired winning goals from Con Martin and Peter Farrell. His presence in defence also steeled his fellow players and enabled them to withstand the massive pressure exerted by England. Maturing in the role of captain, he continued to be selected for his country up to his last appearance, against Austria, in March 1953. Along the way he impressed virtually every international player he played with, including Luton Town's Seamus Dunne, who played alongside Carey in 1952 and 1953.

'My father had died a couple of days before my first international, against France,' Seamus Dunne recalls. 'Jackie Carey and some others came to the funeral. I thought it was great of them to come. Everybody who knew me thought it was wonderful. I didn't even really know these lads at this time. But I remember Carey went around my relations and sympathised. They were saying what a nice fellow he was for doing that. He didn't know anything about me. I had only just met him a few days earlier. I appreciated that a lot.

'Then the day of the match, my first international, I was in the toilet spewing my guts up. I was ashamed of my life that any of the lads might come in and catch me. But I remember Jackie coming in and he was having a pee. He then waited for me to come out to see how I was. I remember it well. He said to me: "How are you feeling?" I said: "I feel awful, my stomach is turning, I'm after throwing everything up." It was a bit of steak or whatever we had before the match. So he said: "You'll feel better after that. You're after having a rough few days. But don't worry about it; this is one of the biggest days of your life. We all had to go through the very same thing. Don't you worry; we'll look after you." He appreciated the fact that it was my first international and it was that more than anything that I was keyed up about. I thought it was very nice of him.

'I also played with him in his last game, against Austria. It was my second international. He played centre-half in both those games. He was very solid. But at that time he had good players there to cover him. We got by with Carey with his experience. He was a good player although not as good or as skilful as he was years earlier. But his experience and tactical know-how and vision were great. He'd shout to me if I was losing concentration and getting on the wrong side of the winger or whatever. From that point of view he was a great tactician.

'Before one of those matches Jackie, who was the most senior player and captain, was giving us a bit of a talk. He said: "Right, lads, the main thing is to try and play a bit of football out of defence. The forward line isn't very big. So keep it low and give them a chance." But when we were under pressure what did Jackie do but give it a big kick up the field. I can remember looking at him. I was only the new boy so I didn't say anything to him. But I could see by the smile on his face that while he was getting a bit beyond it he wasn't going to have any fancy stuff.

'He also was the first person to get the marble shamrock. The FAI presented a shamrock after 25 games. After his twenty-fifth international they presented it to him. It was a massive thing, a Connemara green marble shamrock. But he was the best around when I played with him. He weighed up the game terrifically. That for me was his biggest asset.'

Jackie Carey's career at international and club levels came to an end in 1953. By then he had appeared 29 times for his country. He also had turned out on seven occasions for Northern Ireland, playing at a time in the latter half of the 1940s when dual representation was permitted. His departure from Manchester United was, by all accounts, an emotional affair marked by a unique invitation to join the directors in the boardroom, where they paid their respects to one of the greatest legends in the club's history. Such an honour was rare indeed at Old Trafford.

Following his departure from United, Jackie joined Blackburn Rovers as manager, where he steered the club to promotion from the Second Division in 1958. He later took over at Everton, where in 1960–61 he brought them to their highest League position since the war. Subsequently he moved to Leyton Orient, where he won promotion to the First Division. He then joined Nottingham Forest as boss, before ending his managerial career back at Blackburn Rovers. Carrying with him his fame as a player, he was able to build a sufficient reputation in management to remain in the game up to the turn of the 1970s. Year after year newspapers speculated on when he would return as manager to Old Trafford. Unfortunately, it wasn't to be. With Matt Busby resolutely refusing to relinquish the manager's chair, the return of Jackie Carey died a death.

'I don't think he was a brilliant coach,' Noel Cantwell says. 'Not many brilliant coaches came out of Old Trafford at the time. But people had respect. They knew that the man was a great player himself. It was a bit like Busby; people respected him. He had the authority and he looked like a man who knew something about football. I thought, and most people thought, that one day Johnny Carey would come back to manage Man United. I don't know why it didn't happen. I couldn't tell you. Sometimes it's a matter of circumstances and luck. If you're at a club and doing very well and things are going well for you and the opportunity arises, then you might get it. But because Matt Busby stayed on, with more and more success, there was never an opportunity for Johnny Carey to come back until it was too late.'

It took until 1969 for the Republic of Ireland to appoint its first formal manager with full control over team affairs. Prior to that, selectors chose teams while so-called managers, who were really only so in name, were appointed to take players for training and to guide them through games. Following his retirement as a player and his appointment to club management, Jackie Carey was a wise and obvious choice for the part-time national job. He readily accepted the offer. Throughout the bulk of the 1950s and 1960s he steered many Republic of Ireland teams through their World Cup and European Championship campaigns. He also won the respect of the players, which was hardly surprising given his pedigree with both Manchester United and the national side.

'When I got there he was manager,' Noel Cantwell, who played for and later captained the Republic of Ireland, says. 'I remember when we were training for my first international, which was against Luxembourg, he took part in the little practice that we were having. It was a little five-a-side. We did a bit of running and we did a bit of sprinting. Then you end up by playing five-a-side or six-a-side or seven-a-side. He played in the game, in one of the teams. I thought he was probably the best player that was playing that day. I thought that instead of being manager this fellow should be playing. He was that good and he did it so easily and so simply. He was a great example to anybody.

'He was manager in a part-time capacity. I think he approached it in that sort of way. He didn't go into it in great depth. The FAI at the time was made up by people from Bohemians and Drumcondra and elsewhere. It was difficult to get things done. They didn't have much money. They just selected a team and put the jerseys and shorts and socks out for everybody. I think John used to come over from wherever he was manager, whether it was Leyton Orient or Blackburn or wherever. I'm not sure even if he had much of an influence on the selection of the team. It was very much in a part-time capacity.

'He had a very quiet way of going about things. He didn't shout and bawl. He very rarely raised his voice. He modelled himself on Busby and Busby didn't raise his voice. Busby didn't swear. I never heard Johnny Carey or Matt Busby swear. He was astute. He would tell you something and if you had the intelligence to take it in you could take it in. If you hadn't the intelligence it would just go over your head. He explained what could happen and what should happen in a game and then he left it to us. He also realised that sometimes we were inferior to the opposition. But I always suspected that he was doing the job in the sense that tomorrow he'd have to go back to England and do his real job.

'If he had been offered a full-time manager's job with Ireland it might have been different. But I remember talking to him about things that could be improved like the shirts, the shorts, as well as our approach to the thing and the fact that when we went abroad there were more officials than players and we weren't treated with great class. I often used to say to him: "It's you, the manager, who has got to go in and fight for us." But I did get the feeling that he felt to himself: "Listen, Noel, it is only just a part-time job."'

'During the team-talks,' Seamus Dunne adds, 'his favourite line was: "Look, lads, I'm here to manage the team. I'm not here to tell you lads how to play the game. You have to be able to play the game or you wouldn't be here. You are the best players your country has. Go out and remember that and play up to that standard. I'll help you as much as I can but I'm not here to tell you how to play." Then he'd go through his defenders telling them things like to keep covering each other and to try and keep it down on the ground while getting it away from goal. It was sensible stuff. He always opened up with that and I thought it was a nice thing. The lads would be sitting there all keyed up. But being told we were the best the country had, we'd be getting a bit taller all of a sudden. For me he was excellent at it.'

'He enjoyed the game being played and he enjoyed the game being played from the back,' Noel Cantwell continues. 'I remember one time at a team meeting he said: "Will the forward line stand up?" I think the forward line was Joe Haverty, Arthur Fitzsimons and Dermot Curtis. Now Dermot Curtis was probably the tallest of that forward line and Dermot, I think, was about 5 ft 8 in. So he said: "Listen, fellows, there's no use banging the ball up in the air and sending it long to these fellows because they won't have a chance. We've got to pass it and we've got to build it." That was his way of playing football.

'He enjoyed me as a defender and he enjoyed Charlie Hurley as a defender because basically we were football people playing from the back. We didn't just bash it down the field. We tried to look for our own players in midfield or drop it into the centre-forward or play it wide. I think he enjoyed that. He didn't enjoy the hustle and bustle. That wasn't Carey's style of game. He enjoyed the pleasure and the beauty of the game as a passing game and as a repositioning game. He didn't really enjoy what he saw in Dublin sometimes, namely the up-and-under, somebody charging, which the Irish public seemed to love. He would have preferred us to pass the ball and play it. That was his approach to football.'

'His talents were as a footballer,' Philip Greene says cryptically regarding Jackie Carey's managerial career with the Republic of Ireland. 'He liked to keep to himself when he was manager of the Irish team. He would rather be with me and one or two of the press fellows than with the team. He'd come out with me for a drink or for dinner. Or he'd join someone else. But he stayed away from the players, which I thought was a bit strange. I suppose you can become too familiar and he maybe decided to keep himself apart.

'His philosophy was to "funnel back in defence". That was a mistake, especially in the 1957 match against England. That was one particular match that I was broadcasting and as far as I'm concerned he made the wrong decisions. You should never let players go right up to you, certainly such a clever player as Tom Finney. And that was something Jackie Carey allowed.

'We scored after three minutes, a goal by Alf Ringstead, and we led 1–0. Time was up when the ball was switched across to Tom Finney. Finney went down the stand side. The three biggest men we ever had all confronted him. First of all there was Pat Saward, who was left half-back. Finney beat him. Noel Cantwell was left full-back and Finney beat him on the line. He crossed. He beat Charlie Hurley. The keeper, Tommy Godwin, didn't come off his line, which was the only mistake he made. The ball and Finney with it should have been put over the roof of the stand. But they kept letting them come on. I would have to blame Jackie Carey for that. It was not a decision I agreed with.'

To fully appreciate the stature of Jackie Carey as a player and captain one need only look at his role in the legendary Great Britain versus Rest of Europe game played in 1947. It was billed as the 'Match of the Century'. It was contested in front of 135,000 spectators at Hampden Park. Stanley Matthews played for Great Britain. Jackie Carey was selected as captain of the Rest of Europe. That honour alone indicates his standing in football at the time and the respect he commanded from his peers. It was a tribute that would long be recalled when Jackie's career came up in conversation. It also was much commented upon in 1995 when, at the age of 76, he died, leaving behind memories of one of the finest players ever to wear the red of Manchester United or the green of his country.

'He was such an immense player,' Philip Greene concludes. 'There are always arguments over who is the best player you ever saw. A lot of people go for the tricky footballer. But he was just a monumental player who was good in every facet of the game. He was a natural footballer. He knew when to tackle. He knew when to transfer the ball. He knew where to put the ball. He was a giant next to everybody else, no matter how good they were. I never saw him having a bad game. So when we talk about this, that and the other player I don't think anybody could compare with his record. From the day he began to the day he retired he was just immense.'

3. NOEL CANTWELL

THE CLOSING SECONDS OF THE 1957 INTERNATIONAL BETWEEN THE REPUBLIC OF Ireland and England at Dalymount Park were the most excruciating in the history of Irish soccer. It was a vital World Cup qualifier, with Ireland requiring a win to have any chance of reaching the finals in Sweden. England needed a draw. Ireland led from the opening minutes following a goal by Alf Ringstead. They had further chances to increase their lead. The atmosphere inside the ground was electric. Listeners to Radio Éireann were rigid with apprehension as the final whistle approached.

With the seconds ticking away, the referee looked at his watch. Then tragedy struck. Tom Finney crossed from the wing. Standing on his own was John Atyeo, who headed the ball into the net. The referee blew the final whistle with the score at 1–1. Radio archive recordings reveal the extent of shock in the ground. The hush was deafening. Witnesses would later say that the silence could be heard all the way from Dalymount Park to Nelson's Pillar.

At the core of that unprecedented disaster were two players who would in time become legends. There was Noel Cantwell, who was then with West Ham United and who would later play for Manchester United. There was Charlie Hurley, who was then with Millwall and who was winning his first international cap. Both were larger-than-life characters. Both turned out to be wonderful players. Yet on that day in May 1957 both played central roles in what was one of the most sickening setbacks in the history of Irish soccer.

'That's probably the most disappointing game I've ever played in,' Noel Cantwell remarks. 'I remember prior to the game the excitement, the demand for tickets. It was one of the few occasions that the FAI got us together for two or three days. Usually we got together after mass on Sunday and that was it. But they took us to Bray, to the International Hotel, for three days. It had to be something very special for them to do that because they didn't have any money.

'We were training across the road from the hotel, at the Carlisle Grounds. I remember the state the ground was in. The grass was long. There were no nets. They knew we were coming to train but I'm sure the poor old groundsman did nothing special just because it was the Irish football team was there. It was like a ploughed field. I was asked to take the training. I said: "OK." I got a few little ideas together and I made it as exciting as possible. Invariably they finish in five-a-side matches and a little bit of a light-hearted joke. But before the finish of the coaching session I said to Charlie Hurley: "Charlie, I'll give you some heading practice."

'Charlie was a wonderful header of the ball. He was 6 ft 3 in. and immaculate in his dress and immaculate in every way. He looked at me and said: "Oh, no, not the day before the game. I did my hair this morning and I don't intend doing it again before tomorrow." He also looked at the footballs and they were like lumps of coke. They were big, dirty old balls and he thought to himself: "I'm not going to head one of those because otherwise I'll have to shampoo my hair and get my hairdryer out and everything." So that was the end of that session. We never got around to the heading practice.

'On the day of the match we played very well but they got a goal right in the last minute. I remember it distinctly. England had beaten us at Wembley 11 days beforehand. I had played against Stanley Matthews at Wembley but they had dropped Stanley Matthews for the return game in Dublin. They brought Tom Finney from outside-left to outside-right. It was something else to play against both Matthews and Finney of England in 11 days.

'I remember Tom Finney saying to me about a minute from the end: "Noel, congratulations, you deserve to win the game." We were still in the heat of battle. The ball came to Finney. Pat Saward came over and tried to get the ball from him. Anyway, Finney got to the line and I got back to tackle him. The ball hit the top of the laces in my boot and they lifted the ball over Tommy Taylor and Charlie Hurley. Standing at the far post was John Atyeo. He was probably the worst player on the pitch on the day but there was no substitution and he headed it in.

'You could have heard a pin drop. We picked the ball out of the net, sent it off and that was the end of the game. They got the necessary 1–1 draw. It was the most disappointing game I've ever played in. There was a wonderful atmosphere. I think there were 47,000 there. But it's still spoken about now in Ireland with lots of regret.'

Noel Cantwell emerged in the early 1950s from Cork soccer, where he played with Western Rovers and Cork Athletic. Recommended to West Ham United, he quickly established himself at the Second Division club. In 1953 he made his début for the Republic of Ireland, playing in a 4–0 win over Luxembourg. A natural leader and a versatile player, he was in time elevated to national team captain, a role in which he displayed the same driving, inspirational qualities he was already exhibiting at club level.

Having won the Second Division title in 1958, the media spotlight inevitably focused on West Ham United in their subsequent League campaigns. In 1959 – the year after Manchester United suffered their tragic loss at Munich – the London club came a creditable sixth in the old First Division. Much of their success was due to the towering performances of Noel Cantwell, a man who could play with power and conviction anywhere from defence to the centre of attack. Inevitably, Matt Busby came knocking when he sought to rebuild Manchester United in the wake of the Munich disaster. Noel moved to Old Trafford in 1960, where Busby hoped that his leadership and character would inspire a new and evolving Manchester United side.

'Matt Busby had a big rebuilding job to do,' Noel says. 'Although there were some exceptional kids there, they were still only kids. Matt must have thought: "I've got to get some experience in there." He bought Maurice Setters and he bought Pat Crerand. He bought myself and he bought David Herd. But it was a difficult period for the people at Old Trafford because they still had the memories of Duncan Edwards, David Pegg and all the rest.

'I found it difficult at Old Trafford to start with because there was very little coaching done at that time. You had your Bobby Charltons of the world, your Dennis Viollets, your Albert Scanlons. You had people who had wonderful individual ability. But as far as the team player was concerned, it was more difficult. I didn't know where everybody was on the pitch. At West Ham I invariably did. But they were far better players than we had at West Ham and the atmosphere was incredible.

'The first year or two there, we didn't play very well. We weren't a very good team. Our performances weren't good and it was a cliquey sort of place. You had the old school and you had the kids. The old school might have resented new people coming in. We had a bitty sort of team. Bobby Charlton could do it all right. Then he got Denis Law in, who made a hell of a difference. And during that time he was still bringing on some great little youngsters.

'I remember George Best arriving when he was 15 and he was a spindly little lad. You could see then that he had exceptional balance and he had the ability to beat people. He wasn't strong enough to compete with the bigger boys or the bigger men. But he was an exceptionally skilful player. George came to Manchester and he got homesick. He went back home and he came back again. I remember Matt telling me later on that he offered George's mother and father a house in Manchester, to bring them over to make sure they could look after their son. He could see an exceptional ability. He could see that this fellow was going to be something special.

'In 1963 we won the Cup and I happened to be captain. It was a great day. Leicester were favourites to win it. I think Leicester were going for the Double. But we always played in flashes and we always thought that Wembley would suit us. It would be a day when the Laws and the Charltons and the Crerands would play very well. We had beaten Southampton in the semi-final and Wembley was a guaranteed 100,000. It was a lovely day and things went well for us. We played well.

'Pat Crerand was a star in midfield. Johnny Giles played on that team, as did Albert Quixall and David Herd and Denis Law. Denis played exceptionally well. It really was a day when everything came together and we won the Cup. I happened to be lucky enough to be captain. I think I had only taken over the captaincy early in that season. The turmoil at the club was reflected in how many times the captain changed. But that was a very special day at Wembley.'

There is a famous photograph of captain Noel Cantwell exuberantly raising the FA Cup aloft after Manchester United's 3–1 victory over Leicester City in 1963. A goal from Denis Law and a brace of goals from David Herd had laid the ghosts of Munich to rest. The historic march of Manchester United, which had been so dramatically interrupted by the crash five years before, was back on track. Noel Cantwell had led the Reds from the ashes of Munich back to the pinnacle of football success.

As Noel's club career blossomed in the early 1960s so too did his role in the Republic of Ireland side. Those were years when the national team battled in vain for respectability as an international force. The organisational set-up was underdeveloped. Arrangements were less than inspired. The team was a mixture of players from top-flight clubs, the lower divisions and the League of Ireland. In fact, ever since Noel won his first international cap in 1953 up to his final cap in 1967, the national structures were poorly prepared for the increasingly professional pressures of international football.

'Joe Wickham, who was a lovely man, was secretary,' Noel recalls of the FAI during his years playing for the Republic of Ireland. 'Joe used to phone you up or else you'd get a letter to say you were selected. The itinerary would tell you to bring your own soap, your own towel, your own everything. You would report at a certain time and that was it. You made your way and then you got your expenses after the game. We were getting £50 for an international match in those days and they'd give you a cheque for £45 and they'd give you £5 in cash. That was the deal. Then you'd make out your expenses and if you were very lucky they would pay maybe a taxi. Occasionally they would query your expenses and you wouldn't get them, they'd be too much. That was the scene in so far as the financial situation was concerned.

'The shirt that we used to play in was more like a rugby jersey. As for the shorts, I don't know who they ever thought played for Ireland. They'd put Johnny Giles and Joe Haverty into size 44 shorts. In the dressing-room sometimes they'd pull the shorts over their heads. Occasionally you'd see Giles with a rolled-up pair of shorts and it tucked in like a great, big, baggy thing. How the poor fellow would ever play in it! Joe Haverty was a tiny, little man and it was the funniest thing to see Joe in an Irish strip. We had to put up with that for a while. We got to the stage where fellows like myself, who felt better in better gear, brought our own shorts. Charlie Hurley would bring his own shorts too. We wouldn't accept it.

'Charlie Hurley and myself and Pat Saward would go over on the boat occasionally. They couldn't afford the flights in the early days so we'd go on the boat on the Saturday night and if the crossing was bad we didn't get that much sleep. Then we would check into the Four Courts Hotel, which was where we stayed. We had three or four hours' sleep and then we'd go down with our boots and everything else to the Gresham Hotel and assemble there at 12 o'clock.

'I remember one time we were having a team meeting at say 12.30, having a poached egg or something like that, and Shay Gibbons, who was centre-forward, wasn't there. Johnny Carey was waiting to conduct his team-talk and there's no sign of Shay. Shay arrived at about 1.15 and Johnny Carey, who never raised his voice, said: "Well, Shay, did you know what time the meeting was at?" Shay says: "Yes, I did, boss, I did. But I went to mass and I didn't realise it was high mass." If it had been ordinary mass he'd probably have got out at about 12.20 but because it was high mass it was 1 o'clock. So we had to wait for the priest to finish the high mass. That was the atmosphere.

'Johnny Carey was the manager. He was a lovely man. But John wanted peace and quiet, he didn't want to upset anybody, he just wanted to smoke his pipe and he enjoyed the game. All he ever said to you was: "Fizz it about. Fizz it about." He loved passing the ball. Johnny would look at the team and you'd have Joe Haverty, you'd have Dermot Curtis, you might have Arthur Fitzsimons. The biggest one might be 5 ft 7 in. Then he'd say: "Right, lads, do you know what we've got to do? We've got to get this ball up in the air and charge in there!" It was good fun.

'At that time there were only players born and bred in Ireland and that was difficult. We always had the nucleus of a team but we just didn't have enough to make a very good team. We gave it our best shot. We weren't expected to do too well. We played in Poland. I know Poland well. The Eastern Bloc countries were the only ones who'd play us. We used to play friendlies against them. I remember playing in Poland and they gave us all this Polish money. But once we left Poland it was no good to us. We were invited to the Eastern Bloc but nowhere else.'

Although he was known primarily for his work as a defender, Noel Cantwell also was able to spearhead the attack. This he did for the

Republic of Ireland when a strong presence was needed up front. Nowhere was the tactic more effective than in the crucial World Cup home qualifier against Spain in 1965. Ireland still had hopes of qualifying for the World Cup finals to be held in England in 1966. On the day, Noel frightened the life out of the Spanish goalkeeper Iribar, with the result that the Spaniard threw the ball into the back of his own net.

'I played centre-forward against Spain,' Noel remembers of that famous match at Dalymount Park. 'I thoroughly enjoyed playing centre-forward. At that time, when we played in Dublin, we played with the backing of a good crowd. Our approach to the game was very much a physical one and a direct one. It suited me as a centre-forward. If the ball was banged down the park and I could charge after it, I could put people under pressure. You could frighten the Austrians and the Spanish because they didn't like that. They played for Real Madrid and all the best teams like Barcelona, but when they came to Dublin on a bumpy old pitch it wasn't the same, especially with very little backing from their own supporters. So one of the things I used always do is sort of let the goalkeeper know that I was around.

'Anyway, in the game against Spain there was a cross that came in and I ran at the goalkeeper. He was just about to catch it and I ran at it and I was shouting at him. I can't tell you what I shouted because it wouldn't be fair. I'm about a yard away from him and I'm still shouting at him. I knew I wasn't going to get there and I knew that literally I'd have to foul him to do anything. He just decided to push the ball over the crossbar. He was sort of looking at me as I was coming in at him. And he pushed it straight into the back of the net. We won 1–0. Interviewed after the game, he was asked about the centre-forward. He said: "Loco, the man's mad, he's a bull and he's mad." Now I've never considered myself mad. It was just one of those things. I knew the crowd. The crowd always liked a thing like that in Dublin. You wouldn't get away with it in Spain. I probably would have been sent off. But I knew where I was.'

Towards the end of his career at Old Trafford, speculation was rife that Noel Cantwell would become the next coach and eventual manager of Manchester United. His leadership qualities, understanding of tactics and friendship with Busby were seen as significant. Noel was a close confidant of the manager, with whom he discussed training techniques and match strategies. United, at the time, relied on talent to win games and paid scant regard to coaching. Yet here was a towering figure, a natural leader, respected in the dressing-room, who was already inspiring the players at training. It seemed to observers that his future at the club was assured.

'I remember Matt telling me that he wanted me to be the coach at Old Trafford,' Noel says. 'We went on tour somewhere and I had a whisper from the physiotherapist Ted Dalton: "When we go back you're becoming the first-team coach at Old Trafford." I was very excited because I had sometimes taken training when somebody was missing and I always had in my mind that the training could have been better and more exciting and more interesting for players. But it never materialised. The reason was, I think, that although Matt appreciated me and thought I knew something about the game and that I could lead men, he didn't want to upset the balance of the club, the Jack Cromptons, the Jimmy Murphys and the rest of them. I think he might have thought: "Bringing this young upstart in might just upset the rest of us so we'll leave well enough alone." So he left well enough alone.'

The accession of Noel Cantwell to chairman of the Professional Footballers' Association was, in itself, testimony to his stature in the game. He resigned that role, however, and he also left Manchester United in 1967 to become manager of Coventry City. There he took over from the legendary Jimmy Hill. In the following years he showed his mettle with the club, steering them to sixth in the First Division in 1970 but eventually being sacked in 1972.

'I kept Coventry in the First Division in the late 1960s and early '70s when honestly I believe that most of the teams that were relegated were better than Coventry City,' Noel reflects. 'The chairman sacked me. His secretary came around one Sunday afternoon at five o'clock and said: "Mr Cantwell, here's a note the chairman wants me to deliver." I opened it up and it said: "Dear Noel, this is the most difficult letter I have ever written but you're sacked." So I was doing nothing until somebody at Peterborough asked would I consider coming to Peterborough. I looked at the table and Peterborough were the bottom club of the 92. I took over and I got them away from the re-election position in the first season and then the next season we won the Championship. It was probably one of the most exciting times for Peterborough that they've ever had.'

In his time at Peterborough, Noel Cantwell became something of a legend with the club and to this day he is recalled with affection by fans and players alike. He later moved to America, where he coached before returning to run his pub business back in Peterborough. Further involvement at management level with his local team made up the remainder of his career as a club boss. However, it wasn't as a manager but as an inspirational captain of West Ham United, Manchester United and the Republic of Ireland that Noel Cantwell will always be recalled. More than any other player, Noel epitomised that exciting period in soccer when he led Manchester United back to football success and his Irish team came close to making it to the World Cup finals held in England in 1966.

'When I look back, I've captained every team that I've ever played for,' Noel concludes. 'Given the ability I had, I think I extracted as much as I could out of it. I was always one of the lads but then when it came to the football side I was very serious. I don't think looking back that I could have achieved much more than captaining West Ham and to be associated with people like Bobby Moore, who was a dear friend of mine. I was lucky enough to be captain at Old Trafford. And then, of course, there was the great fun of playing for Ireland even though we really couldn't win very much.

'I've never thought about how I'd like to be remembered. I feel now that some of us, like the George Bests of the world, we're all remembered as better players than we were when we were playing. I would think I had good leadership qualities. I was enthusiastic but limited in ability. But I have very happy memories and great pals. I'm still very welcome at all the grounds that I've ever played at and I've got lots and lots of friends in the game.

'We have good get-togethers at Old Trafford and we have good get-togethers at West Ham. Unfortunately, there are far greater financial rewards in the game of football today. But I never look back and say to myself: "Oh, my God, why wasn't I born later? Why couldn't I be a Denis Irwin or a Roy Keane?" They had both come from the same place as me. I've had a very good life and a good, happy family life as well. So, all in all, I'm very happy about my little contribution to football.'

4. JOHNNY GILES

IN THE 1950S A DUBLIN TEENAGER TRAVELLED WITH HIS SUITCASES TO MANCHESTER United. This was no schoolboy outing to Old Trafford. Nor was it a weekend excursion to cheer on his heroes in a League or Cup match. Instead, this was a venture into one of the epicentres of football in England – a city where wisps of smoke hung over housing projects during winter Saturday afternoons and where men donned heavy coats and woolly underwear to witness one of the finest teams in soccer history.

Back in those days Manchester United was the home of the Busby Babes. Slowly evolving and maturing through the mid-1950s, they gradually set the world of football on fire. By 1956 and 1957 they were winning League titles. They also were progressing in Europe, competing with teams like Real Madrid, Anderlecht, Borussia Dortmund and Atletico Bilbao. This was fantasy football 1950s-style. And into that football shrine in Manchester stepped a quiet, shy schoolboy from Dublin who was clearly destined for greatness. His name was Johnny Giles.

'Billy Behan was scouting for Manchester United and he was a friend of my father's,' Johnny says. 'Billy had been watching me and there was a connection with Manchester United early on. I actually went to Manchester when I was 14 for a holiday. They used to call it a holiday in those days; it was a connection with the club. I wanted to join Manchester United anyway because I followed them mainly through Johnny Carey and the 1948 team and then the Busby Babes. I wanted to go to Manchester and Billy Behan was actually watching me for probably three years before I went over.

'It was unbelievable for a young lad going to Manchester. I was only 15. It was a wonderland of football. You went pre-season training. All the players trained together, young players, old players. You'd be with Tommy Taylor, Duncan Edwards and Bobby Charlton. You were seeing them first-hand. There was such a terrific amount of talent playing in the first-team versus second-team games. I couldn't believe the amount of talent that was there.

'You played at your own level. I was only 15 and I was very shy and a very self-conscious type of young fellow. I didn't mix in very easily. I always had confidence in my football but I wasn't very confident in anything else. I played for the lowest team when the matches started. I played for the youth team. They didn't want to put me into the "B" team, which was then the fourth team. I think they felt I was a bit small, a bit fragile. I'm not very big now and I wasn't big for my age in relation to the English lads. But I always felt I was OK. I was strong enough, that was the main thing.'

As the autumn of 1957 set in, the cold, frosty weather was kept at bay by the warmth of football produced at Old Trafford. These weren't ordinary matches against ordinary teams, featuring ordinary players. Instead there were lively, competitive home games with Blackpool and Spurs, a derby with old rivals Manchester City, away battles against Wolves, Preston North End and West Bromwich Albion. Dukla Prague and Red Star Belgrade came to visit. In early October Shamrock Rovers played at Old Trafford in the first round of the European Cup. A third consecutive League title seemed inevitable. The prospects for success in Europe never looked better.

On display at Old Trafford were some of the finest stars of the day. England internationals Duncan Edwards, Roger Byrne and Tommy Taylor linked up with Ireland's Liam Whelan and Harry Gregg. The young Johnny Giles lived in their shadow. That shadow, however, would darken immeasurably on 6 February 1958 when the Busby Babes were virtually wiped out on a snow-covered airfield in Munich. On that awful day the lives of Tommy Taylor, Liam Whelan, Eddie Colman, David Pegg, Geoff Bent, Mark Jones and Roger Byrne were snuffed out. A few weeks later Duncan Edwards died from his injuries. Johnny Giles, left behind in Manchester, was shocked to learn of the crash.

'I was playing in the youth team at the time,' Johnny recollects. 'We were down training at Old Trafford on the day of the crash. Bill Inglis was an old trainer there and he was looking after us. He came in when we finished training and said that the plane coming back had crashed. We didn't think it was serious. We thought it was something that had happened on take-off. Nobody knew what the news was at that time, during the early hours of it. It was only when I went back to the digs and the news came through that we realised how bad it was.

'There was a dreadful atmosphere around the club at that time, as you would expect. It was a dreadful tragedy. The club was a very sad and dreadful place at the time. It changed Manchester United completely, I think. The atmosphere before Munich was of young lads growing up together. They hadn't bought many players. There were only about two or three players that they bought and the rest were young lads who had come up together. That gives you a special atmosphere in a club because there are no outside influences. They had just won the League two years on the bounce. You could see them dominating for years. Then after the Munich air disaster they had to buy players into the club. It was never the same again. It couldn't be because you got older players coming in, outside influences, and the whole atmosphere of the club changed.'

It took until 1959 for the teenage Johnny Giles to make the breakthrough at Manchester United. His début for the first team was in a match against Spurs staged at Old Trafford. Munich survivors Bobby Charlton, Harry Gregg and Bill Foulkes togged out for United that day. Albert Quixall, the new golden boy in the team, was missing, replaced by the young Giles. The outcome, a 5–1 defeat, was disastrous. For Johnny Giles, however, the die had been cast and he was back in the team the following month. That season alone he made 10 appearances for the first team. He also was selected for the Republic of Ireland international side, winning his first cap, against Sweden, in November 1959.

'I had played two matches in the Manchester United first team when I was picked to play for the Irish team,' Johnny recalls. 'In those days we didn't have that big a selection of players; we didn't have the qualification rule. Anybody that showed anything like getting into Manchester United's first team had a good chance of getting into the Irish international team. So I made my début in November, just short of my 19th birthday and it was brilliant.

'It was great because only a few years earlier I was going up to

Dalymount Park to see the international team. Heroes of mine were playing in it like George Cummins, Dermot Curtis, Noel Cantwell, Charlie Hurley, Pat Saward and Mick McGrath. I used to go to Dalymount Park with my pals to watch them and suddenly, from nowhere, you're in the dressing-room getting ready for the match beside them. So that was brilliant. It was something I'll never forget.

'We played Sweden and Sweden had just beaten England on the Wednesday. This was 1959. Sweden had been in the World Cup finals in 1958. They were a very good side. Most of the lads had played on the Saturday and had travelled over. That's what they used to do in those days, play on the Saturday and travel over for the Sunday. We got off to a terrible start. We were 2–0 down. Then I scored and Dermot Curtis scored two goals and we finished up winning 3–2.'

On the club front, Johnny Giles' career blossomed in the following four years and it seemed to observers that another Irish recruit would follow in the legendary footsteps of Jackie Carey and Liam Whelan at Old Trafford. Johnny was steadily notching up first-team appearances when the oddest of events occurred. Although a member of the FA Cup-winning team of 1963, when United defeated Leicester 3–1 at Wembley Stadium, in the late summer of that year he was unexpectedly let go by Matt Busby.

'The feeling was mutual,' Johnny says of his departure from Manchester United. 'I wanted to leave because I felt I'd have a better future somewhere else. Matt Busby didn't want me to stay. I think it went back to 1962. I was playing inside-forward and we got to the semi-final of the Cup. Bobby was playing on the left wing. I was the main schemer, as they called them in those days, and I played very badly. I had a really bad game against Spurs. They beat us 3–1 and beat us comfortably. I think Jimmy Murphy and Matt Busby lost confidence in me after that. I hadn't played well and I think they thought I wasn't going to do it.

'There was a definite loss of confidence because they bought Denis Law during the summer. So I was moved back out on the right wing the following season. I felt during the 1962–63 season that whatever I did, I couldn't do right for doing wrong. By the end of the season I wasn't happy at the club. I played in the 1963 Cup final and I played in the matches in the Cup. I played in almost all the League matches.

Then we played in the Charity Shield the following season and got beaten by Everton. I was left out straight away. I went to see Matt and said that I felt it was better for me to go. And he didn't disagree.'

In August 1963 Johnny Giles made the unexpected but fortuitous move from Old Trafford to Elland Road. At the time Leeds United were languishing in the Second Division, having been relegated from top-flight football back in 1960. A bargain-basement buy, Johnny linked up with a team that was showing progress and ambition under manager Don Revie. They won the Second Division Championship in Johnny's first season. Immediately, they went on the hunt for First Division honours, narrowly missing out to Manchester United in their first challenge for the League title. Despite that initial success, few observers could have predicted just how effectively Leeds United would perform in the years ahead.

'I knew Don Revie was a very ambitious man,' Johnny recalls of his transfer to Leeds United. 'He came to see me. When you go on the transfer list, as a player you wonder every day if anyone is ever going to come in for you. I was only on the transfer list a couple of days when he came in for me and spoke to me. I was impressed with him. He was one of my idols as a player.

'One of the main reasons I went to Leeds was that Bobby Collins was there. Bobby was a great player, another hero of mine, and I knew he was doing his stuff at Leeds. There were lots of young players there. I didn't know them very well but you just have a feeling about a club. I'd rather join a Second Division club trying to do something than a First Division club who weren't trying to do anything. Obviously I never knew in those days that Leeds would be as successful as they were. But the fact that they were signing me meant that they were spending money. I think Don Revie came to see me on the Wednesday and I believe I signed on the Thursday morning.

'Bobby Collins was great and I learned a lot from him. There was a great drive about him to win matches. In dressing-rooms with Bobby, I've seen it when we've had a few players out missing through injury and Bobby believed he could win the match. He really believed that he could win the match no matter what team was playing. I saw us draw matches or win matches where normally you wouldn't think you'd have a chance. I learned from Bobby that any team I played in should expect to win.

'Norman Hunter, Billy Bremner, Paul Reaney, Peter Lorimer, Eddie Gray and Terry Cooper were all at the club at that particular time. Don Revie was a great influence on those players. He'd be out training and putting them right along with Syd Owen and Les Cocker. If they made a mistake on a Saturday they'd put it right on the Monday in training. That was different from Manchester United. Matt didn't come on the training-ground in those days. If you lost he'd say: "Unlucky, lads." But he wouldn't do anything about it for the following week. Matt believed: "Get the players in and let them do it." At Leeds, Don Revie couldn't afford to do that. He built a good atmosphere at the club. There was a good attitude, people learned the stuff, learned the basics, learned to defend properly. They were young lads and they were very good. There was great drive about them. There was a good team spirit. And we got promotion that year, in the 1963–64 season.'

Over the next 10 years Leeds United became one of the finest teams in the history of English soccer. They won the League Championship in 1969 and 1974 and were runners-up on a further five occasions. They won the FA Cup in 1972 and were runners-up three times. They won the League Cup in 1968. They won the Fairs Cup in 1968 and 1971 and were runners-up in 1967. Finally, they were European Cup Winners' Cup runners-up in 1973 and European Cup runners-up in 1975. Without any doubt, the team were the most consistent force in English soccer up to the mid-1970s, battling at various times teams like Manchester United, Manchester City, Derby, Arsenal, Everton and Liverpool for League supremacy.

'I think it was one of the best teams that ever played in England,' Johnny remarks. 'First of all, to have a great team you have to have great players. Once you get the great players in, you've got to have the right attitude. The right attitude is the will to win, players looking after themselves, going anywhere in the world and giving a performance, not backing off against anybody, playing for each other and playing for the team. I think Leeds had all of that. The only weakness was Gary Sprake in goal. Gary let us down a few times. I spoke to Don before he died and he said that he did have a blind spot about Gary. Don had a sense of loyalty. But I think he played him too long in the team.

'What happened with Don as well is that seasons roll into one and he didn't realise that the players were getting older and better. He still maintained the same attitude as when they got in the team. He paid maybe too much attention to the opposition when we became a great team. Shankly, for instance, with Liverpool, had a different approach. He'd say: "You're a far better team. You'll kill them. You'll wipe them off the pitch." He built his team up. Don never did that. If we were playing Sheffield United, on the Friday he'd have a meeting and he'd go through the Sheffield United players. If you didn't know them, you'd think they were a great team. His attention to detail is what made Leeds good in the first place. That was his style.

'Again I spoke to him before he died, when he wasn't well, and he said that he didn't see the team growing up because one season rolls into another. Time goes by very quickly in football and the lads who needed that control and attention to detail became great players after seven or eight years. We were together for a long time. I think we became a really top-class team around 1968–69. And we became a great team, I think, in '69, '70, '71, '72. I'd be biased, of course, and people will say: "Well, you're biased because you played on the team." But I've spoken to people who were in the game, who weren't connected with Leeds, and they felt that it was one of the best teams they've ever seen.'

In the latter half of the 1970s Leeds United stayed in the upper reaches of the First Division although their days as title contenders were gone. By 1982 the club had slid to the Second Division and the great years of the 1960s and 1970s were well and truly over. In 1975, following the club's defeat by Bayern Munich in the European Cup final, Johnny Giles departed for new pastures. At first he joined West Bromwich Albion where, as player-manager, he led the side to promotion from the Second Division. After a notably successful spell managing in England, he returned to Dublin where he took over at Shamrock Rovers. Although he secured the FAI Cup in 1978, the dream of turning Shamrock Rovers into a breeding-ground for young talent and a powerful football force never quite took off.

'I wanted to do something that hadn't been done before,' Johnny reflects. 'I could have stayed in England. West Brom offered me big money to stay. I was the only manager in England at that time who had left a successful position. I went back to Shamrock Rovers to try and bring on young players in Ireland, to keep them at the club, to keep them in Ireland, eventually to go on from there and hopefully do well in Europe. It was a big dream that didn't work. But I think the principle was right. There are lots of young players in Dublin but I found it very difficult to keep them. I can understand if lads are interested in England. I was the same myself when I was a young lad. If English clubs come in, they go to English clubs. But what I tried to do in principle was right.'

On the international front, the name of Johnny Giles became an automatic selection following his first appearance, against Sweden, in 1959. Throughout the 1960s and 1970s he featured in all of the Republic of Ireland's great campaigns including battles in Moscow, Berlin, Vienna, Liege, Ankara, Seville, Montevideo, Santiago, Copenhagen, Glasgow and Poznan, not to mention appearances at Wembley Stadium in London and Dalymount Park in Dublin. From 1973 to 1980 he also managed the national side, steering the team close to qualification for the 1978 World Cup finals and bringing a new level of professionalism to the international set-up during his time in charge.

'The main thing, when I took over the job as the Irish manager, was to get away from the inferiority complex of those days,' Johnny says. 'I always got the feeling that it was OK for everybody else to do it but it wasn't OK for us to do it. Over the years we had loads of moral victories because people expected that. We went away and were beaten 2–0 and it was a good performance, a moral victory. What I tried to do in the Irish team, more than anything else, was to get away from that. Nobody ever expected us to qualify for European Championships or World Cups. Players didn't expect to do it. What I did, when I got in, was to raise the expectancy. It was my own downfall in the long-run because after three or four championships they said: "Ah, Giles is no good. He's had three or four attempts at qualifying for championships and we haven't done it."

'We were very close. We had a couple of dreadful refereeing decisions in Bulgaria and France. But people don't want to know about that. To people, you either do it or you don't do it and we were very close to it. The team was getting better. We had a great selection of players because of the qualification rule. It opened up a bit from previous times and we got very close on a couple of occasions. When I took over the job people never expected us to qualify. I raised the expectancy, which didn't do me any good personally in the long-run but I don't mind about that.'

When footballers discuss the all-time greats of Irish soccer, the name of Johnny Giles gets special prominence. The quintessential playmaker, he used his vision to control and orchestrate games. As a midfield general he inspired fellow players with his tireless endeavour. His passing was immaculate and his goal-scoring prowess was remarkable. Although he played and managed at the highest level, his career in football was a long one – encompassing two full decades at international level, from his first cap in 1959 to his last cap 20 years later in 1979. Few players from any part of the globe could boast such a rich and prolonged career in the game of football.

'I was very lucky,' Johnny concludes. 'I had ambitions going into the game as a young player to play in England and win things in England, which I did. I feel very privileged and very lucky to have done that. I played in a great team and I got great satisfaction from it. I did almost all the things that I wanted to do in the game. So I had no regrets when I finished playing. I didn't have it in my blood that I wanted to play longer and longer. I'd had enough.

'The next step after playing was management and I never enjoyed management. If you're in management and you're away on holidays you're still preoccupied because you know there are things to do. No matter what stage you're at in football you can do better so you're always looking to improve. I got to the stage where I wanted to have my mind open and free to do the things that I wanted to do myself. I was around 44 or 45 when I thought: "I'm not going to live until I'm 90. It's very unlikely." So I wanted to spend the rest of my life away from football.

'Football has been great to me. Football was my life. Coming from a working-class area, if I didn't have football what did I have? I wasn't good at school. I didn't like school. I was very lucky in that I achieved most of the things that I wanted to achieve. There are very few people who can actually say that. I wanted to be a professional footballer; I became a professional footballer. I wanted to play for Ireland; I played for Ireland. I wanted to win a Cup medal. I wanted to win a League Championship medal. I wanted to play with great players. I wanted to play in a great team. I did all of that. I feel very lucky to have been able to do it and very privileged to have realised dreams that I had when I was a young boy. So if you ask me if football was good to me, the answer is it's been great to me.'

5. ALAN KELLY

THE YEARS SPANNING THE 1950s AND 1960s WERE CHAOTIC ONES IN IRISH SOCCER.
Throughout that era, Republic of Ireland internationals based in
England travelled by overnight boat to play in home internationals.
They dashed from Saturday afternoon matches in places like
Birmingham, Manchester, Preston and Blackburn to catch the
Liverpool sailing. Carrying overnight bags, they battled stormy seas
and vomit-ridden passenger ferries in the hope of arriving at Dublin
by sunrise. Some missed their connections. A few never turned up.
Others came late. The lucky ones made it to the pre-match Sunday
lunch and the bus to Dalymount Park. How they then battled the
cream of world football, one can only guess.

At the time, conditions for the Republic's international footballers
were less than ideal. Team get-togethers were rare. Tactics were
primitive. Back-up facilities were virtually non-existent. Moral
victories – better known as narrow defeats – were the norm. Friendly
internationals invariably were played against Soviet-controlled
Eastern Bloc countries. Yet, despite such deprivations, a succession
of Republic of Ireland sides produced some remarkable results,
defeating the likes of 1954 World Cup champions West Germany
while featuring players of world-class calibre and renown such as
goalkeeper Alan Kelly.

'We used to come off the boat after playing on a Saturday in
England,' Alan Kelly, the Bray Wanderers, Drumcondra, Preston
North End and Republic of Ireland goalkeeping legend, recalls. 'The
planes weren't leaving after half past seven or eight o'clock at night,
and some of us couldn't reach the airport. So we used to travel over
via Liverpool on a Saturday night and land in Dublin on the Sunday
morning at seven o'clock. Then we'd go up to the Gresham Hotel

and we might be playing against Italy or France or Spain on Sunday afternoon. We accepted it and that's the way it was.

'I remember in the Gresham one Sunday, we were eating our pre-match meal about 12 o'clock or half past 12 and there were seven of us at the table. Someone said: "Where's the rest of the fellows?" One of the lads said: "I remember someone saying something about the Four Courts Hotel." I can't remember who made the phone call to the Four Courts Hotel but sure enough the other seven were up there having their pre-match meal. There had been a little bit of a mix-up in the arrangements. Anyway, the coach went up to the Four Courts Hotel and then picked us up at the Gresham and off we went to Dalymount Park.

'I remember another story as well. Mr Carey was the manager. We went to Austria. There was a great player named Willie Browne, who played for Bohemians, and he was only an amateur. We arrived in Vienna on the Sunday and it was hammering down with rain on Sunday, Monday, Tuesday and Wednesday. We were just getting ready to go out. Willie Browne was in front of me and Mr Carey was standing to the right. He said: "Willie, can I have a look at your boots?" Willie said: "Yes." Willie showed him his boots and he only had rubber, flat-soled shoes. Mr Carey said: "Willie, you won't be able to stand up out there. The place has been swamped, there are pools of water." And Willie says: "Well, that's all I have." Willie had such a big foot that nobody else's boots could fit him. Anyway, we went out. We drew 0–0. And Willie Browne came in off the field and his white shorts were still white when he came in. He was probably the best player on the park. Sometimes, nowadays, we think: "Remember, that happened to us."

'We were always in Poland and we couldn't figure out why we were always in Poland. But one of the committee members' friends had a business in Poland, so I have more Polish caps than any other caps. Czechoslovakia was a favourite place for us as well. We were always behind the Iron Curtain and we always enjoyed going there. We became the local team after a few years because we were over there so often. We always had great memories of going to those countries.

'There was one particular memory we had. We were in the hotel in Prague and we'd lost a couple of the lads. They were out walking on Tuesday and apparently they'd gone into some shop to buy something. They couldn't speak English over there and the lads had just picked up something to look at and the police had got them and we didn't know where they were. In the end, we got them out about two hours before the game. Little things like that happened to us. But they were a great bunch of lads and the memories will last forever.

'I also remember Joe Haverty, when we played Spain, and Joe had a little bit of an injury. He went out and played and he was playing well. All of a sudden he pulled up after about 20 minutes or 25 minutes and he just waved his hand. Nobody knew why. Joe had swollen glands right in between his legs. We just kept saying to him: "What's wrong, Joe?" He was pointing to where they were and he couldn't walk. We had such a good laugh about that. It wasn't laughable for Joe, who was in agonising pain. But Joe is very small and very quick and very sharp, and with the thought of him running we had a big laugh about that. But we always felt that we did go out and have a go. Some of us had bad times and some of us had good times. But we always tried to pull for each other and help each other.'

Back in the early to mid-1950s the foundations were laid for the remarkable goalkeeping career of Alan Kelly. From the humble playing-pitches of Bray, County Wicklow, he progressed initially to Bray Wanderers and then to League of Ireland giants Drumcondra. Those were great days in the history of Drumcondra, where Alan tasted his first success by winning an FAI Cup medal. He also was knocking on the door of the international side. For the first time in over five years, the selectors chose a home-based goalkeeper for the friendly at Dalymount Park against West Germany in 1956. The name of that goalkeeper was Alan Kelly. For the record, Ireland beat the reigning World Cup champions 3–0.

'I can only remember doing one good thing in it,' Alan recalls of that first international appearance in November 1956. 'I remember one of their players broke away and I was lucky enough to smother the shot. Otherwise, I didn't have much to do that day. I didn't have much to do because the players in front of me were so good. Noel Cantwell got one of the goals. I think Joe Haverty got one of the goals. Lucky for me, I kept a clean sheet. I was probably walking on water anyway after being in the League of Ireland for about three months or so and then getting picked for Ireland. I didn't even play in the League team, which generally you had to go through first. But West Germany were 1954 World Cup champions and a 3–0 victory for us made for a great day.'

Within six months of his successful début against West Germany, Alan Kelly's career took a downward turn. Chosen to play in the Republic's next game, against England in May 1957, he had what can only be described as a nightmare. The match, a critical World Cup qualifier, was at Wembley Stadium. England lined out with Billy Wright, Duncan Edwards, Stanley Matthews, John Atyeo, Tommy Taylor, Johnny Haynes and Tom Finney. Although high on confidence after their previous victory, the outcome for Ireland was nothing short of disastrous. A hat-trick by Tommy Taylor and a brace of goals from John Atyeo secured a 5–1 victory for the English. It would be almost five years before Alan Kelly would get another chance to play in goal for Ireland.

'It was a nightmare day for me,' Alan recollects. 'I remember being interviewed in a newspaper the week before and I just casually said: "Well, I've no nerves going to Wembley." I remember reading it in the paper and I thought to myself: "I shouldn't have said that." I mean, you walk out at Wembley and you're playing against a team with a forward line of Stan Matthews at outside-right, Tom Finney at outside-left, Tommy Taylor the great Manchester United centre-forward playing up front, Duncan Edwards in the middle of the park, Billy Wright at centre-half, Johnny Haynes and Johnny Atyeo, all these great players. It was an Irish paper I said it in and I thought: "I shouldn't have said it."

'The game got going and I can remember one of the goals. I remember coming out to catch a corner-kick about seven yards out. The next thing I remember was someone lifting me up by the shoulders. It was Noel Cantwell and I was behind the goal line. The ball was in the back of the net. I could see the white shirts of England going back towards the centre line. I just remember saying to Noel: "Is it a goal?" He said: "Sure is." I said: "What happened?" He said: "He's knocked you in the back of the net from seven yards out." That's the way it was in those days.

'I then went on and made a few more mistakes. We eventually lost 5–1 and I probably should have saved two or three of the goals. I had to try and pick myself up after that and just carry on with the job. In that game I can remember everything that happened to me. I maybe made one or two saves but I don't remember them. I remember all the mistakes I made and I didn't sleep too healthily for a week or two.

'The return game was in Dalymount Park. I think it was two weeks after. They picked the team and understandably I wasn't selected. Tommy Godwin took my place. They trained out at the International Hotel in Bray and I was invited out to meet the team. The game was on a Sunday and I finished up paying at the turnstiles to go in and watch the game from the terraces. It just goes to show that you can be up one day and down the next day. After that, I had to live and learn.'

In 1958 Alan Kelly was transferred from Drumcondra to Preston North End, where he became a legendary figure. The club had a long and distinguished history, having won the very first League Championship in 1888–89 without losing a game while winning the Cup the same season without conceding a goal. Subsequently, however, their fortunes had slid somewhat, although at the time of Alan's arrival they were still riding high in the First Division. From the time he was elevated to the first team up to his retirement, he made a record 447 League appearances for the club and became one of the great figureheads in the history of Preston North End.

'I don't think it was a big transfer fee,' Alan remarks of his move from Drumcondra to Preston. 'It might have been a couple of shillings. But it was still the best thing that ever happened to me. I was a plasterer by trade and you would swap getting up at six o'clock in the morning in the building trade for getting up to train and play soccer while getting paid for it as well. I thought how lucky I was to be transferred to Preston North End.

'When I went to Preston North End they were top of the First Division. Fred Else was a terrific goalkeeper. Tommy Docherty played. Frank O'Farrell, who was a big favourite in Ireland, was there. The great, big Willie Cunningham played for Scotland. They were a great side and I had to wait three years to get on the first team, although I had two international caps when I went over there.

'At the end of the third year I said to Jimmy Milne: "Look, Fred Else is a great goalkeeper. There's not much of a chance for me here." He said to me: "Listen, Alan, you're doing all you can. But Fred is looking for a £5 rise. If the Board agree to give it to him, you'll be going to Liverpool." Now Fred Else was worth a £55 rise in those days. But as the Board didn't agree to give Fred the £5, I took his place in Preston North End's team and Fred got transferred to Blackburn Rovers.

'The game was a lot more open at the time. Nowadays everything is closed down. Everything is marked tightly. But the big difference when I started at Preston North End was that we used to play with a leather ball. If you could kick it 30 yards you were a superman. It used to get wet and laces were in the ball. When the players headed the ball they'd have an imprint of a lace on their forehead. Nowadays you can whiz a ball 60, 70, 80 yards because of the difference in the texture of the ball.

'The ball made a great difference in those days because the ball didn't travel as fast and players had a little bit more time. It was a lot more open. That helped in the sense that good players became great players because they had more time on the ball and a bit more open space. I'm absolutely amazed the way the ball pings about nowadays. But I was privileged to play against some of the greatest players in England at national level and League level.'

The high point of Alan Kelly's career at Preston North End came in 1964 when the club reached the FA Cup final against West Ham United. It was a thriller of a game between two sides committed to playing stylish, open football. On paper, the match promised to be a one-sided affair. The reality was entirely the opposite. Having taken the lead twice, Preston ended up being beaten by a goal scored in the dying seconds of the game. It was one of the cruellest endings to a match that could just as easily have gone Preston's way. As it happened, they lost to West Ham United by the score of 3–2.

'The pinnacle of anybody's career is to go and play at Wembley,' Alan says. 'We had a good football side and were always renowned for playing good stuff. We beat Swansea in the semi-final. We went on to the final against West Ham, who were a great football team as well. John Sissons, Bobby Moore and Johnny Byrne played for them, to name but a few. The system in those days was a lot freer and a lot more open. We weren't afraid because we knew they were a good football side and we thought: "Great."

'We took the lead and then they equalised through John Sissons.

Then big Alex Dawson got a header and we were 2–1 in front. Geoff Hurst equalised for them in the second half. It was ding-dong up and down the ground. Then, with seconds to go, their right-winger got down the line, cut in and passed across. Ronnie Boyce from West Ham came along and buried it with his head and they were in the lead 3–2. Our lads were on their knees by then. West Ham won the game 3–2. But the most vivid memory I have is when we all got on the bus going back to the hotel, all the players plus coaches were crying. We could see our families outside. They were waving to us, and all that. We got over it as the night went on. But I always say it was the most I've ever seen of an accumulation of people all crying at the same time. It just goes to show what the game is all about – the feelings you get when it doesn't work out. But, of course, the feelings you get when it works are great as well.'

After a club record 447 League appearances and 126 clean sheets, Alan Kelly's career came to a close at Preston North End. Apart from the FA Cup final appearance in 1964, they weren't the most successful years in the club's history. In fact, they dropped out of the First Division in 1961 and fell to the Third Division in 1970. They won the Third Division title in 1971 but within a few seasons the career of Alan Kelly was over. It happened quite tragically in a game against Bristol City.

'I remember a shot came into the right-hand, bottom corner,' Alan recalls of that match. 'I dived and I caught the ball. But my elbow jammed in a little bit of a divot in the ground. My shoulder jumped up and I just started screaming. I held onto the ball. Nobby Stiles, who was playing on that Preston team, said: "Hold your hands out, you can't hold onto the ball." And he just booted the ball out of my hands for a throw-in. The trainer ran on and it was a bad dislocation. They took me off and it was discovered that I had damaged the nerves in my arm. I was paralysed for about three months and they couldn't operate on me. The staff at Preston did everything they could for me. They were brilliant. The specialist said: "Let's just see how it goes." After about four months my muscle on the top of my arm gave a little bit of a twitch and it eventually came back. I tried playing for a year but I couldn't reach the standard I wanted. So I had to finish. I had my arm back and moving but I had to retire.'

In 1973 Alan Kelly played his last game for his country in a 1–1 away draw with Norway. A lot had changed since the late 1950s when he lined out alongside players like Liam Whelan, Alf Ringstead, Pat Saward, Arthur Fitzsimons and Peter Farrell. So many new players had come and gone in the intervening period. The last international line-up he played with featured players like Ray Treacy, Don Givens, Mick Martin and Paddy Mulligan. It was a measure of Alan's longevity that he had survived such an extended period at the game's highest level.

In the years to come, his name would live on through his sons Alan Kelly Junior and Gary Kelly, who both became goalkeeping stars in their own right. Alan Junior began with Preston North End before moving to Sheffield United and Blackburn Rovers. His other son Gary was best known for his years playing in goal with Oldham. The Kelly family were something of a unique dynasty, performing at various levels for their country and keeping the family name alive in the game of soccer for almost half a century.

'Alan and Gary did great,' Alan says. 'I have another son, David, and he played in goals for an amateur team in Preston. So Gary was a goalkeeper, Alan was a goalkeeper, David was a goalkeeper and I was a goalkeeper. They've always looked to making themselves better. They've done a lot on their own. They've worked hard at it. I might have helped with bits and pieces but in the main they've done it themselves. I'm really proud of the three of them. But we always say the best goalkeeper in the family is Mary, my wife.'

By the time he retired from football, Alan Kelly had accumulated 47 caps playing for the Republic of Ireland. Later he worked with the national side under Johnny Giles and he even managed the side for one match – a 2–0 victory over Switzerland in 1980. His name is revered at Preston North End, where he officially opened the Alan Kelly Town End as part of the stadium development at Deepdale. Above all, however, he left behind memories of a consistent, reliable goalkeeper who, although capable of dramatic saves, acted as a dependable last line of defence for the Republic of Ireland in the 1960s and early 1970s.

'It feels like a million years ago,' Alan says of his years in goal for Preston North End and the Republic of Ireland. 'In those days there was a lot of comradeship. Everybody was really good friends with each other. That's not to say that on the field if something didn't go right they wouldn't raise their voice at you. They would. They'd let you know. But in those days there were lots of lads who sort of knocked around with each other. They were pals with each other. That was true especially at Preston, where the whole team knocked around together. We trained together, we played together and we went out together.

'I made a lot of friends and I enjoyed the game. But I think the biggest thing was the comradeship that we had. If someone was having a bad time, we got in behind him because it might be our turn next week. There was a lot of that. That was one of the big things that stuck out for me: how friendly the people were, how much help I've had, how much I enjoyed the game, and I hope I gave both to the Irish people and the people of Preston a little bit of pleasure watching me.'

6. GEORGE BEST

IT BEGAN LIKE A STORYBOOK ADVENTURE. THE YEAR WAS 1961. THE DESTINATION WAS Manchester. Transport was by overnight boat to Liverpool. The last lap of the journey was by train. It was summertime. Many passengers were visiting relatives in England. Others were returning after a visit home. But two of those passengers were on a date with destiny. Alone, unsure, lonely and filled with apprehension about what lay ahead, their ultimate destination was one of the homes of British soccer – Manchester United.

That day in July 1961, 15-year-old George Best left Belfast in the company of Eric McMordie. Both were heading for trials at Old Trafford. From Liverpool's Lime Street station they travelled by train to Manchester. No one was there to meet them. They paid for a taxi. Having asked to be taken to Old Trafford, they ended up at the cricket ground. The error rectified, they finally completed their journey. At United's training-ground they were introduced to Northern Ireland legends Harry Gregg and Jimmy Nicholson. They were then brought to their digs. And so it was, overwhelmed and exhausted, that the young, skinny, waif-like George Best embarked on one of the finest careers in soccer history.

'I was playing for the local youth team Cregagh Boys and also for my school team,' George recalls. 'The guy who ran the boys' club, Bud McFarlane, got in touch with Bob Bishop, the Manchester United scout. Because I was so small and skinny they arranged a game for me against some bigger boys, some 17-year-olds, to see how I would do. I scored a couple of goals in the game and they contacted Matt Busby and said: "We found this kid, we'd like to send him over." So I went over with another lad, Eric McMordie, and we only stayed for a day and a bit. We came home because we'd never been outside of Belfast before, except to Bangor. So my dad contacted Matt Busby. He thought we might have got in trouble. But Mr Busby said: "There's no problem. He's only homesick. If he wants to come back we'd love to have him."

'I returned to United and eventually made my début at 17 against West Brom. There was a crowd of something like 54,000 at the game. The atmosphere was amazing. I'd only found out a couple of hours before kick-off that I'd be playing. Graham Williams was left-back for West Brom. He was a very uncompromising full-back who played for Wales. He gave me a couple of whacks early on. Matt Busby decided for the second half to move me to the other wing, to keep me out of the way of this mad Welshman.

'Then a couple of months later I made my international début. Coincidentally it was against Wales at Swansea and Graham Williams was the full-back again. He gave me another couple of whacks in that game. Fortunately we won both games. I saw him not so long ago at a dinner and I said: "This is what I look like from the front."

'In those days I was playing between 70 and 80 games a season. I was in the youth team that won the FA Youth Cup. I was in the first team. I was playing for Northern Ireland. I was playing a few games in the reserves. I was playing at least three games a week. In that first season, on a Saturday I played a First Division game at Old Trafford. Monday night I played at Swindon in the first leg of the Youth Cup final. Wednesday I played for Northern Ireland in Belfast. Thursday we played in the second leg of the Youth Cup final against Swindon. I was upset because we didn't have a game the following Saturday. I wanted to play every day because I loved it so much.'

In George Best's first full season with Manchester United (1964–65) the club won the First Division title for the first time since 1957. Two years later (1966–67) 20-year-old George Best was again in exhilarating form and United were champions once more. To seasoned professionals like Bobby Charlton and Denis Law it was clear that a rare football talent had been discovered. Here was a player of slim physique, with nimble skills, playing one-twos off opponents' legs and embarrassing opposition defences with his trickery and his skill. He was also scoring breathtaking goals.

The world's media were drawn to this handsome teenager whose

Beatle haircut and good looks had caught the imagination of the public. He was soon a magazine pin-up, modelling clothes, frequenting clubs and discos and causing hysteria wherever he appeared. He dated models and actresses, with his image forever appearing in the press. With Best on the wing and in the news, United became the British glamour team of the 1960s.

'The era, at that time, was changing,' George says. 'The music was changing. The fashion was changing. Most of the music side of it was in the north of England. I had a lot of friends in the music business. I used to go and watch them in concerts. They used to come and watch me play. But there was no pressure early on. I was a normal kid. I was doing something I loved and getting well paid for it.

'I suppose I was the first. It was the first time they'd seen a player with hair down to his shoulders. When I first started they thought my Beatle haircut was long. It got a lot longer later. I remember when we had to go abroad, to places like Albania or Russia, I was like a freak show. They'd never seen anything like it. All these mad clothes, big multi-coloured shirts with the big lapels and high-heeled boots, and hair twice as long as they'd ever seen before. Also I was modelling. Footballers had never done that before. I was in pop magazines. It was interesting, to say the least.

'We were also winning everything. Matt Busby had this knack of blending together so many different characters. We all had totally different characters, Denis, Bobby, myself, Nobby Stiles, Paddy Crerand, Bill Foulkes, Alex Stepney, Shay Brennan. We were all individuals. But he taught us that we were all together for the one cause and that cause was Manchester United.

'Then, after 1966, the "El Beatle" thing began. We beat Benfica 5–1 over there and they christened me "El Beatle". I was 19 at the time and I had gone over and destroyed them. The media coverage was huge. I was followed around constantly, 24 hours a day. They didn't want to write about the football. They wanted to write about everything else I was supposed to be doing. That's when the pressure started from a personal point of view.'

Both Manchester United and George Best reached their peak in 1968 on the turf at Wembley Stadium. On that glorious May evening, United became the first English club to win the European Cup, beating Benfica of Portugal 4–1. That victory marked the culmination of a long, hard journey, the climax of an adventure that began with United's European ventures in the 1950s and that cost so many lives on a snow-covered runway at Munich Airport in 1958.

'We always felt that we were going to do it; that we were going to win the European Cup,' George remarks. 'The players who had been at Munich, like Bill Foulkes, Bobby Charlton and Harry Gregg, always felt we were going to be the first English side to win it. By 1968 we had that nice blend. We had a few younger players in the side plus great experience. We were very, very confident.

'For weeks before the match I had planned all the things I was going to do, all the tricks I was going to play. It didn't work out in the 90 minutes. Then, in extra time, I scored a goal. I stuck the ball through the centre-half's legs, after a long clearance from Alex Stepney. When I went through I knew I was going to score. It was a question of how it was going to end up in the back of the net.

'In that split second when everything seemed to stand still, I had decided to take the ball around the keeper and stop it on the line and head it in. I changed my mind because the silly old bugger got up and chased back to try and stop it. When I watch it now I still think he's going to catch it, he's going to get a hold of it. We then scored another couple of terrific goals and it was all over.

'When it finished everybody's first thoughts went out to the boss. Mine certainly did. He was the first person we looked for. All the boys wanted to keep their shirts but I'd been asked by almost all the Benfica players to exchange mine. I ended up exchanging with, I think, Coluna. So I was the only person with a white shirt on in the lap of honour. I kept it for years and years and then gave it away to some kid in hospital. Then we went up to collect the trophy. After that I remember nothing.'

Following the European Cup victory, Manchester United hosted a lavish celebratory banquet at the Russell Hotel in London. Understandably, United's manager Matt Busby was overcome by emotion and, following the dinner, he sang a tearful version of Louis Armstrong's 'What a Wonderful World'. Club captain Bobby Charlton, exhausted by the evening's game, retired early to bed feeling dizzy and unwell. Veteran Paddy Crerand sat on the hotel's stairs discussing the future. But one of United's finest stars from the game was missing. George Best, scorer of the extra-time goal that had broken Benfica's hearts, was nowhere to be found. To this day he has no recollection of where he went.

'I don't remember what I did afterwards,' George admits. 'I remember coming off the pitch and going down the tunnel but after that absolutely nothing. I know we had a celebration banquet somewhere. I found out later from other people which hotel it was in. I think I went out to a nightclub in London, owned by a friend of mine, and I had a few drinks with him. That's what I planned before the game anyway so I suppose that's where I ended up. I probably staggered home to the hotel about six o'clock in the morning.'

Few observers of that evening in 1968 could have predicted the path that Ireland's greatest football export would take in the years ahead. A week prior to the final George had turned 22 and was the undoubted star of a Manchester United side that had set European football alight. His grace, speed, balance and breathtaking ball control had caught the imagination of the football world. The embodiment of the 'Swinging Sixties', he owned a boutique in Manchester and his affairs with attractive models and starlets featured prominently in the British media.

Selected as the 1968 Footballer of the Year, European Footballer of the Year and ending the season as the English First Division leading scorer, it seemed the future possibilities were limitless. Having conquered Europe the challenge facing United and Best was to build on that success and emulate the triumphs of Europe's finest clubs such as Real Madrid. Unfortunately it was not to be. Within six years Manchester United were relegated to the old Second Division and Best, who was drinking heavily, had departed in disgrace from the club. Ironically for George Best that European Cup final had marked not the beginning of something great but the first step in a downward spiral ending in alcoholism, imprisonment and a premature departure from the football stage.

'After the victory in Europe I started having to hide from the press,' George recalls. 'They were parked outside my home 24 hours a day, looking for whatever they could get. I was getting assaulted in places by nutters and lunatics. I'd stop at traffic lights and people would walk past my car and spit on it or bang the side of it. My car was constantly being scratched or had paint thrown all over it. If I wanted to go out with some friends to see a show, I had to call the theatre and sneak in when the lights had gone down and sneak out later. I can't remember a show or a play I saw to the end. It became like living in a goldfish bowl.

'The team was also beginning to break up. Bobby Charlton was getting towards the end of his career. So also were Bill Foulkes and Paddy Crerand and Alex Stepney to a lesser degree. Denis Law moved on as well, to Manchester City. We were going out against average sides and being beaten. I think Chelsea came to Old Trafford one season and hammered us 4–0. We had always done well against Chelsea, myself in particular. In games where we should have pulverized teams, we were winning nothing and sometimes not even getting close. It was sad that such a great side disintegrated so quickly.

'I stopped enjoying playing. I hadn't been used to losing. Even when I was a kid at school we won almost every week. I didn't mind losing if a team outplayed us on the day but it was constantly happening. I wasn't happy with it and I wasn't happy with the signings that weren't being made. A lot of very good players, like Alan Ball, had become available. I thought he was the type of player United should have broken the bank to get. Instead the club made some bad signings that weren't up to the standard Manchester United always had. I was becoming a little bit disillusioned with the whole thing. Once I stopped enjoying it, I just felt that it wasn't right to carry on.

'I remember the day it finally came to an end. I had walked out a couple of times and by then Tommy Docherty had taken over. Paddy Crerand was his assistant. They came to me and said: "Come back and do extra training and get yourself fit." That's what I did. I went back and trained in the morning. When all the other players finished I went back in the afternoon and did extra training. Then we played I think it was QPR the week before a Cup match. It was the first time I felt I was getting close to what I wanted to be. I was going past people again.

'The following week we were playing Plymouth at Old Trafford in the Cup. I thought: "This will be my chance to show that I'm back to my best." I trained on the Monday, Tuesday and Wednesday, two sessions a day. I didn't go in on the Thursday morning but I trained instead on the Thursday afternoon. I went in on the Friday and

Tommy Docherty didn't mention the fact that I hadn't come in on the Thursday.

'Then, on Saturday at about 1.30, Tommy Docherty called me into the referee's room. Paddy was in there as well. Tommy said: "You're not playing today." I basically said to him: "Well, if I'm not playing today against Plymouth then I'm not playing again." He walked out and Paddy stayed back. He said: "You'll feel different on Monday." I said: "There won't be any Monday."

'I didn't watch the game. I stayed in the players' lounge. They scraped through, 1–0. I stayed for a while after the match and I had a few beers with the boys. Then I went up and sat in the stands for about an hour, I suppose, after everybody was gone. I never went back to play for United.

'I shouldn't have retired. It was the circumstances. I wanted to play football but I only wanted to play for Manchester United. I didn't want to play in the Second Division. I didn't want to play against teams that were beating us. So I took what I thought at the time was the easy option. I stopped playing. I could have played for another English club but Manchester United was the only club I wanted to play for. So I became a gypsy. I took my boots all over the world.

'I ended up in Los Angeles. When I went there I could walk down the street. I could go to the supermarket, take the dog for a walk. I could walk along the beach in California and not get bothered by anybody. It was lovely. It was heaven for me. I could go into restaurants and not have some lunatic throwing a drink over me. If you're a personality in Britain, whether in music, theatre, films or sport, the media put you on a pedestal and think they've got the right to knock you off. They do so very quickly. In the States they put up with anything as long as you're doing it on the pitch or in your particular field. It was wonderful for seven years.

'Unfortunately the drinking got serious, deadly serious almost. When I first went to America the football was brilliant. The crowds were massive. I had a great lifestyle but a lot of free time, which is not good. Eventually I moved from Los Angeles to Fort Lauderdale where I had a bust-up with the coach so I ended up in San Jose. My wife at that time, Angie, and I were living like gypsies. I've lost contact with how many different homes we had over that period.

'When we moved to San Jose we had a lovely house but the area was a little bit adrift from anything. The nearest shopping mall was about eight miles away and the nearest pub was about six. I started drinking really heavily and we were on the edge of divorcing. It was inevitably going to happen because I would disappear for days on end. I wasn't eating at all. All I wanted after getting up in the morning was a drink. It didn't matter if I had to walk six miles to get one.

'I got arrested once and I went in for treatment. I had a month in hospital, had the treatment and kicked the booze for a year. Yet I knew in the back of my mind that sooner or later I was going to have another drink. I went back for another treatment for a month. I tried implants. I tried to take a pill every day.

'Eventually I came to London where I went for counselling. They promised no one would find out about it. I couldn't go to AA because "anonymous" I wasn't. So I tried this private clinic in London where I went on a daily basis. The press found out about it. So every time I went there the press were waiting for me outside, hoping to see me fall in or fall out. It was just a matter of keeping going and finding a solution.'

In the early 1980s George Best returned permanently to Britain from America, leaving his wife Angie and their son Calum behind him. Following his arrival in Britain he was pilloried and pursued by the press. His bouts of binge drinking and his public indiscretions became a regular banner headline on the tabloids' front pages. His erratic behaviour finally culminated in a confrontation with the British police resulting, in December 1984, in a three-month prison sentence for assaulting a policeman, drunk driving and failing to answer bail.

'At the time I was having spells where I was drinking for months and other spells when I didn't drink at all,' George says. 'When I did drink it was worse than before I stopped. I was cancelling work. I was not turning up for things. I was letting friends down. I was letting family down. It was a total nightmare.

'Eventually I ended up in Pentonville prison. You can't get any lower than that unless you're dead. I went there and had a good look at myself. I thought: "What the hell are you doing to yourself, what's happening?" The first week or so in Pentonville I was with these guys who had committed all these hideous crimes over Christmas and New Year. Then I went to an open prison.

'We all know what open prisons are like. You can get anything you want, basically. I went and trained four or five hours a day. I had a wonderful girlfriend at the time who came to see me as often as she could. A few friends, like Michael Parkinson, came along to say hello and gave support when I needed it. My poor old dad, imagine what he was going through?

'I came out and I was super-fit. I was probably fitter than when I played my last home game at Old Trafford. I came out and I thought: "I've got to pay everybody back." Eventually I had a conversation with a friend of mine who is a doctor in Manchester. I've known him for a long time. He said to me: "You know, it might sound stupid to you but it's like a light switch. You either leave the lights on or switch them off. You have to decide what you are going to do." And I decided, from then on, that I was going to work hard and get myself sorted out.'

George Best played his last English League football with Bournemouth in the old Third Division in 1983, one of a long sequence of lesser clubs including Stockport County, Cork Celtic, Fulham and Hibernian that employed his talents in his fading years. Having left top-class football he continued to appear in charity benefits and testimonials and turned out briefly for Tobermore United in Northern Ireland in the 1984 IFA Cup. He finally hung up his boots and turned to after-dinner speaking and television commentating, where he has made his living ever since. Despite the turbulence of his personal life in recent years, he is still remembered as a football superstar who played 466 games for United, scored 178 goals, won 37 international caps and whose skills lit up Old Trafford for 12 golden years.

'It's hard to believe so much time has passed,' George concludes. 'I'm still a massive Reds fan. I go to Old Trafford regularly and I'm welcomed by almost all the fans. I went on the pitch recently to draw some lottery tickets and the reception from the crowd was something else. It was like stepping back to when I was 17 or 18. They were absolutely brilliant. So it's great. At the end of the day, no matter what I've done, it's the football that they remember.'

7. TONY DUNNE

THE PSYCHOLOGY OF SPORTING SUCCESS AND FAILURE IS HARD TO FATHOM. TO outsiders the equation is simple. Victory brings euphoria and elation. Defeat results in depression. The reality, however, is frequently different. Take May 1968, when Manchester United became champions of Europe. The overriding emotion was one of relief. Players were overcome with exhaustion. Others were physically sick from the tension. And at least one of that famous European Cup-winning team was plunged into a melancholic state, conscious of the achievement that had just been secured yet lost in a haze of depression.

For Tony Dunne that evening in May '68 ended as a dismal affair. His team were champions of Europe. The tragedy of Munich was finally laid to rest. Matt Busby, Bobby Charlton and Bill Foulkes had emerged from a plane's wreckage to secure the Holy Grail. Yet, surprisingly and inexplicably, the event passed this talented Dubliner by. He stood alone, observing the crowd and his fellow-players, lost in his thoughts, detached from the mayhem at Wembley.

'After the game I really tried to jump with joy but all I could think was: "Christ almighty, thank God that's over, thank God we've won,"' Tony recalls of that famous night. 'Busby was there and you could see him and you knew it was a different planet he was on, his feet were kind of raised. I saw Bobby Charlton and I thought: "God, we've won, it's wonderful, it's absolutely wonderful." But inside of me there's something that's dragging me down and I'm thinking to myself: "Look at that silly twat jumping up there, he's happy." I was trying to jump and be part of it but it was really a low time for me.

'After it was over we went to a function. My father came to the function and he was very happy and he was thrilled and all that. My wife would have been the same; she was happy and really didn't know how to handle me, I suppose. I was half up and half down, trying a few drinks, trying to be happy. If anybody spoke to me I was very polite and delighted, but I was at a low key, I'd have to say. I really would have been better if I could possibly have shuffled around on my own for a while and got a few drinks and maybe got drunk, had a few beers and fell on the floor. It might have been better.

'Don't get me wrong, I was over the moon we'd won and I'd achieved something and we'd broken the barrier for Matt Busby. We were the first English team to win the European Cup and in 10 years he'd done it. The team that was killed in the crash I still believe today would have won the European Cup. We followed on, we won it and I was delighted because we had succeeded for the fellows that had been killed in the crash. I was over the moon, but I was over the moon in a low-key way. And my thoughts at that time were my own thoughts. I felt it was more for something else; it was more for history than for me. When it was done, everybody sort of said: "Thank God the period is over, now we can start living," or something like that. But that's history. Yet it was a lovely time, a lovely time in history and it gave me everything in life.'

In the wake of the Munich disaster of 1958, Matt Busby embarked on one of the most impressive buying sprees in the history of British football. In came players like Denis Law from Torino and Paddy Crerand from Glasgow Celtic. Up through the ranks came Nobby Stiles. But few players matched the value for money of the young full-back from Shelbourne by the name of Tony Dunne. Spotted by United's legendary scout Billy Behan and transferred in 1960, he became the bargain-basement buy of the new-look Manchester United team. Arguably the best full-back in the club's long history, Tony Dunne would in time establish a formidable partnership for club and country with his colleague Shay Brennan. Known for his tenacity and intelligence, he helped United win two League Championships, one FA Cup and, of course, the European Cup in 1968.

'The move to United came out of the blue,' Tony recalls of his transfer from Shelbourne at the age of 18. 'We were playing Shamrock Rovers in the FAI Cup. Matt Busby had been at the game with Billy Behan. After the game I went to the movies with my girlfriend and a message came up on the screen: "Would Tony Dunne please go to the front entrance." Frightened to death I was, I didn't know what was going on. Anyway, I came out and the manager of Shelbourne was there. Gerry Doyle was his name. He was a very keen man who loved his football and he said: "Manchester United want to sign you. I'm going to take you down to see your mum and dad." I said: "Bloody hell."

'I went to see my mum and dad and I said: "I'm going into town, there's a man wants to sign me." "Don't worry, son," my mum said, "if you don't make it you can always come back to us." So I went with my girlfriend and Gerry Doyle to the Gresham Hotel and there was Matt Busby with his wife. He was a big man and he looked an awesome man to me. His wife looked very well dressed and very well off, I wouldn't say snobbish but I suppose a little bit upper class and made me feel quite small. Billy Behan was there as well. "Hello, son, how are you?" Matt Busby said. "I'm fine," I said. He said to Gerry: "The wife will look after Tony's girlfriend and we'll just have a chat over in the corner."

'I went over to the corner and he said to me: "Listen, son, I've watched you play and I think I can make a footballer out of you, make you a professional if you're prepared to take the chance and do what I tell you. What do you think?" "Well, yeah, sure, of course, if you can help me, yeah, that would be great," I said. I was pleased as Punch. He said: "Your club is having a Cup run and they would like to keep you till the end of the season. What we'll do is we'll sign a contract but we'll leave you here till you come out of the Cup." "Oh," I said, "that's marvellous."

'I was an amateur at the time, so he said: "Your manager will sort things out. Your club should get something but at the moment they would have a problem getting something. Gerry Doyle will sort everything out on this side. We're working out a way for monies to be paid to the club and I'm sure he'll see you right." So I said: "Oh, fine, fine," not knowing anything about finances. I didn't realise what was going on. I hate saying these things sometimes these days because they make me feel like a fool, but I wasn't up to it. So I said: "Yeah, OK."

'Anyway, I was signing for Manchester United and Gerry Doyle said: "What you have to do now, Tony, is you've got to sign semi-pro for us." So I signed semi-pro and then they got three grand off Manchester United and they gave me 300 quid, which was a lot of money then. I gave it to my dad and he gave me 100 back. I didn't really know I was going to get any money and I didn't know what 300 quid was. We won the Cup that year, anyway, and I went straight from Shelbourne over to Manchester United.'

Having won a coveted FAI Cup-winner's medal with Shelbourne in 1960, Tony Dunne made the short cross-channel trip to Manchester. There he joined a team that was slowly emerging from the ashes of Munich. Harry Gregg, Bobby Charlton, Bill Foulkes and Dennis Viollet, amongst others, provided links to the tragic crash that had taken place just two years before. New players like Maurice Setters and Noel Cantwell were being drafted in. And virtually straight into the melting-pot stepped Tony Dunne. He made his League début in a 5–3 loss to Burnley in October 1960, having already appeared in a friendly against the great Real Madrid.

'I was sitting on the bench with four other subs,' Tony recalls of that match against the Spanish giants. 'In the second half somebody got injured. Busby came down to the bench and he said: "Strip." I thought he was joking. My gut was running wild. I was half taking my tracksuit off and saying: "Me?" He said: "Yeah, strip and get on there at number three, get on." I said: "Are you sure?" Jack Crompton was pushing me on and my legs were going like 90 miles an hour. I ran on and I always remember this fellow, Canario, who was the right-winger, got the ball and I ran after him like the clappers. I went bang and on the ground he went. The referee gave a free kick. It ended 2–2 and I remember I came off and people were talking about Real Madrid's great teams and I was thinking: "God, I played against them."

'We were playing Burnley the following week. Burnley were a real good team at the time. Anyway, I played against Burnley and I was marking John Connelly. John was an English international then. He was a fiery winger, he was quick, good feet, cool. It was a hard game for me. He taught me a lot that day. I chased him and harassed him and it was hard work. I fought him as hard as I could. I tried everything. I tried getting there early and I tried letting him run. Even though I got the ball at times and did well at times, it was hard all the time. I thought if it's as hard as that for me all the time then I've got a problem. I think we lost 5–3. I felt like he'd won and I thought we got stuffed. I thought if it's as bad as that I can always go and see my mum.

'We became very good friends later on, when he came and joined United. We played in the team and we were room-mates and I used to say to him: "You know, I hated playing against you." He used to say: "What! Don't you remember you used to beat us?" I said: "If we were beating you 3–0 I couldn't wait for the whistle to go. Other times I could accept playing badly and I wanted to stay out to do better. But you I was glad to see the back of." He said: "If you had told me I'd have done better. You always looked like you were coasting to me." I said: "You can forget that coasting bit."

'I have to say John Connelly set the standards for me. He was the main thought in my mind when I played against everybody else. When I went out to play a match my first thoughts were to shut up shop early so that I could help somebody else. I would work through the principle of getting to know the player I was playing against, to know what he did and to try and stop it early. A typical example would be if he was a bit quick and liked to beat you down the right, if you shut that off you would know that after a little while he'd be looking for the ball over the top. That was the one you were looking for too because you were quicker than him. It put me into a thinking mode, which I had never been in before. All I ever wanted to do was not look silly, but now I was thinking of trying to correct things, trying to be as clever as them.'

Throughout the 1961–62 and 1962–63 seasons Tony Dunne became a regular on the newly-evolving Manchester United team. In both those seasons United struggled in the League, languishing in the lower reaches of the old First Division. However, some important developments took place. To begin with, the core of a fine side, with players like Charlton, Brennan, Dunne, Foulkes, Giles, Law and Stiles, began to take shape. In addition, the team showed its potential by winning the FA Cup at Wembley Stadium in 1963, with a strong Irish presence in the form of Dunne, Cantwell and Giles. Slowly but surely, Matt Busby was putting together a collection of players capable of matching the great Busby Babes of the 1950s.

'In speaking to you, he always made you feel that you were the one,' Tony says of Matt Busby. 'He made you feel that you could handle it, you could do it and you couldn't think you were any good until you had achieved. He was a man with so few words. If you played badly and you came off, he'd put his hat on walking out the door. "Cheerio, lads, have a nice weekend," he'd say, "I keep telling everybody you're a great team and then I watch you play like that today and I think: 'Am I a fool?' Have a nice weekend, lads." That was worse than giving you a rollicking because you felt for him and I think he knew that. He left you and all weekend you'd be thinking: "Monday, tackling, training, got to go out and do more running." You could see other players like Bobby Charlton and Denis Law doing things. Everybody was trying to do more.

'I'd be out doing extra running, different runs. Busby would come up and say: "What are you doing? You don't need to do extra training." "I do." "You don't." "I have to. I have got to get it right." "OK, I'll leave it with you. Don't get injured. How are your mum and dad?" "All right." "Tell them to come over soon for a game. See Les, he'll get you the tickets." "OK, boss, thank you very much. Thanks, boss." That's how he reacted. He always asked the right things: "How is your mum and dad?" even if you had forgotten them, which is easy to do. You'd forget them over particular spaces of time. I used to send money home and things like that, but other things take over. Then he reminds you again. He could always say those nice things, but he made you absolutely sure that work, hard work and winning were the only things that were going to make him happy, in particular winning the European Cup.'

In the years prior to Manchester United's famous European Cup win of 1968, the team slowly but surely took on a consistent and formidable shape. In came players like the young George Best. Out went older stars like Albert Quixall, Noel Cantwell and Maurice Setters. The devastating attacking formation of Law, Best and Charlton soon came to prominence. Equally importantly, the back line of Tony Dunne and Shay Brennan settled down and started to gel.

In the 1964–65 season Dunne and Brennan played side by side for the full League campaign. They also lined out together throughout the team's prolonged FA Cup and Inter-Cities Fairs Cup runs that same year. Not surprisingly, United won the League Championship in 1964–65, which was an achievement they repeated in 1966–67. They also, of course, won the European Cup in 1968. The names of the two Republic of Ireland internationals, Shay Brennan, who was born in Manchester, and Tony Dunne, who was born in Dublin, became almost inextricably linked with all those successes.

'I think Shay was a little bit cleverer than me, I suppose more subtle than me. I was more of a tackler,' Tony observes. 'Shay was very mobile and I was very mobile. Shay, being a winger, had a winger's brain as well. I didn't have it as much as him. My thought always was if he was in trouble get it back to me, only to give it back to him again. In doing that you had to keep moving forward. But there were times in a game when you'd end up running with the ball and suddenly it was like somebody had opened the doors. There was only one place to go, which was forward. You keep going and you don't stop to look back. You don't pass the ball back because Busby wouldn't allow you. You hope that somebody will come along so you can just give it to him. As soon as you do that, you turn around and there they are on the touchline saying: "Tony, get back."

'At Manchester United we only had a back four. People forget that. We had Shay Brennan, Bill Foulkes, Nobby Stiles and Tony Dunne. They were our defenders. In front of them you had Paddy Crerand, a beautiful passer of the ball, and Bobby Charlton. They couldn't defend to save their lives, so the lifeblood for them was us. Then you had Best and Law. You just can't get any better. George Best was absolutely magnificent. He used to have two people around him sometimes. What I'd do when George would get the ball, I'd run past him, moving forward, to distract one of the players so they'd end up one against one. Then I'd just head back.

'I could run up and down all day. That was no problem for me. I was quick. I enjoyed running up. Playing with those boys made you feel like you wanted to go out and run up and down. If you could get the ball often enough you could give it to them. In order to do that the only people that had to be organised was us. Everything that stopped us having a problem was brilliant. So we worked together.'

Starting in 1962, Tony also became a regular on the Republic of Ireland international team, making his first appearance in a 3–2 home defeat by Austria in April of that year. His international career was tinged with regret as the team narrowly failed to make it to the

1966 World Cup finals, losing to Spain by a single goal in the infamous play-offs in Paris in November 1965. That team was worthy of better, containing as it did players like Noel Cantwell, Shay Brennan, Tony Dunne and Pat Dunne (all Manchester United), Johnny Giles (Leeds United), Andy McEvoy (Blackburn Rovers) and Mick Meagan (Huddersfield Town). Tony's international career also was artificially restricted, with his modest collection of 33 caps over 13 years being curtailed by Matt Busby's reluctance to release his star defender for international duty.

'One time I played an international and I came back with an injury,' Tony remembers. 'I went to Ted Dalton, who was the physio, and he said to me: "What's the matter with you?" I said: "I've just got this little pull." He said: "Christ, have they rung in? Who rang?" I said: "I don't know, maybe they have. I'll tell you what, just put a little thing on it and I'll go out and do the training." "You wait there a minute," he said, and he came back in with Busby. Matt Busby said: "Tony, what's the matter? Did you get any treatment? I haven't had a phone call. You'd better play tomorrow or there'll be hell to pay." I said: "Yeah, I'll be playing tomorrow." At the time I wasn't too sure. I had a slight pull. I played the next day and he noticed it in the game. After the game he said to me: "I want to have a word with you on Monday."

'I went to see him on the Monday and he said: "How's the leg?" I said: "Ah, it's coming on." He said: "You get treatment for three days. We're not playing till Saturday, but you rest and get it right. I'm going to tell you now, you'll never play for your country again if they don't ring me up or tell me about your injuries. I can't have this. You played with a slight injury on Saturday. I know because I know you. But you won't play for your country again until they get a physio and a doctor and they report it properly. They're running it like a Mickey Mouse club. They can have the others but they're not having you." And that was it.

'I can't understand the reason now as to why he let the others go. Shay might have been in and out of the team at the time, I don't know. But after a game he'd stop me on the way out and say: "Where are you going?" I'd say: "I'm getting the bus with Noel and Shay, we're playing an international tomorrow." And he'd say: "No, you're injured." I'd say: "I'm not injured." "You're injured," he'd say, "get back in there." And he wouldn't let me play.

'It was very hard to speak up to him. He'd say: "You're the best. You're the best because I made you the best. What I want you to do in the team is what I want you to do in the team and nobody's taking that away from me. We have an important game. I'm making sure you're there. If you're there and you do the job I want you to do, we win. How are your mum and dad?" Ah, here we go again. "How's the wife?" "How are the kids?" "Is the house all right?" "Are the windows broken?" It was a club house. "Have a word with Les and he'll get that done." "Make sure you see Les if you want anything done." "Your mum and dad, tell them to ring Les, get the tickets, and take a day off next week. I want you resting next week to give you a chance. Monday I think is a good day. Come in Monday and I'll have a word with you and we'll take a day off." "OK, boss." "Go and sit down and have a cup of tea." And that was it.'

In 1973 Tony Dunne's career with Manchester United came to a close, following which he moved to Bolton Wanderers. It was a mystery to observers why United manager Tommy Docherty ever let him go, especially in view of the new lease of life he experienced at Burnden Park. Freed from the constraints that were imposed by United's playing style, Tony roamed up and down the wings and became a legend all over again in his new club surroundings. By the late 1970s, however, he had finished with Bolton Wanderers and had moved to the USA, where he ended his career.

At Old Trafford, Tony Dunne is recalled as perhaps the finest full-back in the club's long and illustrious history. That alone is a remarkable accolade, especially considering the fine players like Denis Irwin and Roger Byrne, the club captain and England international who died in the Munich crash, who also figured in United's back line. Tony's determination, timing and simplicity of style were remarkable by any standards, helping United win two League Championships and one FA Cup in the 1960s. More importantly, he will always be recalled for perhaps his greatest performance on that night in May 1968 when Manchester United banished the ghosts of Munich. It was a night when the club and its supporters celebrated a great moment in history but, sadly, it was a time when the sense of euphoria was lost on one of the team's star performers, Tony Dunne.

'From 1960 to 1973 was my time with Manchester United,' Tony concludes. 'It was a time of living with great players and trying to achieve. And when I had achieved, I never really felt I had achieved. That sounds Irish but that's absolutely true. I felt like I was trying to climb to the top of the mountain and when I got to the top of the mountain I felt like there must be another hill around here somewhere. Getting there is not always the thing that sets a person alight. It sets other people alight because that's what they're aiming for as well.

'It's a history thing; a team is killed in a crash and 10 years later a team wins the ultimate prize. People wouldn't be wrong to say that the achievement has got me more things in life than anything else. But I would have to say that in terms of feeling as a human being it didn't achieve what I thought it would. I suppose I thought it was the most important thing in life to do what Matt Busby wanted to do, to win it. I wouldn't say I was disappointed. I probably just grew up and found out it wasn't the most important thing in life, maybe.'

8. DEREK DOUGAN

NOT EVEN THE WILDEST OF OPTIMISTS COULD HAVE PREDICTED THE FINAL SCORE. Brazil, after all, were World Champions. They paraded magnificent stars like Rivelino, Jairzinho, Clodoaldo and Paulo César. Their opponents, the All-Ireland XI, were a loose assortment of players from both sides of the border. They had never before played together. In fact, they had just been assembled for this novel occasion under the strange-sounding name of Shamrock Rovers Select XI. Yet they performed with distinction. They also skilfully fought back from 4–1 to 4–3 while pushing the visitors to the pin of their collar. It was a performance that deserved – and received – a standing ovation from the more than 30,000 in attendance at Lansdowne Road.

That day in July 1973, an extraordinary mixture of players lined out for the All-Ireland XI. From Northern Ireland came the likes of Pat Jennings and Martin O'Neill. From the Republic of Ireland came Johnny Giles and Don Givens. Predictably, Jairzinho and Paulo César got their names on the score-sheet for Brazil. Less predictably, Mick Martin and Terry Conroy scored for the home selection. Pat Jennings saved a penalty. But no player performed better than the tall centre-forward from Northern Ireland by the name of Derek Dougan.

In that match Derek Dougan scored his team's second goal. One of his headers was saved off the line. Another wasn't far off the mark. From one of his passes Don Givens hit the crossbar. He had a role in Terry Conroy's goal that narrowed the gap to 4–3. But most importantly he set people talking about how an All-Ireland team could perform with style and conviction against the world's greatest football exponents.

At the time of the match against Brazil, Derek Dougan was riding high with Wolverhampton Wanderers in the old First Division. A devastating goal-scorer, he was hammering them in against the finest defences in Britain and Europe. In 1971 Wolves came fourth in the League. In 1972 they were UEFA Cup runners-up. In 1974 they won the League Cup. And throughout those years, Derek Dougan turned in masterful performances in the Wolves' attack. It seemed inevitable that this East Belfast footballer would rise to the challenge against Brazil, although his role in organising the event angered the Irish Football Association and cost him his international career.

'I got a telephone call out of the blue in early '73,' Derek Dougan recalls. 'It was from Johnny Giles saying: "My brother-in-law, Louis Kilcoyne, is doing a wee bit of work for the Football Association of Ireland. He's been instructed to go over to Brazil and to try and invite Brazil to play. They're coming on this forthcoming tour and would you be interested in bringing seven guys, including yourself, to play them?" I said: "OK, if he can pull off bringing Brazil you can rest assured I'll have six other players and myself." The result was that Louis Kilcoyne came over to my house, confirmed everything and I said: "Louis, shake on it. If you can do that, I'll certainly assist you with it." So I got Pat Jennings, Bryan Hamilton, Martin O'Neill, Allan Hunter, Liam O'Kane, David Craig, and I never had to ask them twice.

'Unfortunately, going 4–1 down I thought to myself: "I don't believe this." Then we clicked into gear in the second half. I got a goal. Terry got a goal. And I still say to this day that if we had another 10 or 15 minutes there's no doubt we'd have overrun them. They'd never really had a guy who was so good in the air and I just kept saying: "Pitch it up, pitch it up, pitch it up." I couldn't believe it. They were jumping on me, pulling me down and I thought: "If this goes on for another five or ten minutes I've got to get a penalty." I was so proud because if we had been beaten 4–1 all the cynics and sceptics could have easily said: "Yeah, we told you so." But we came back. And looking back on it, I'm so dead chuffed that we scored three goals against Brazil.

'They never picked me after the '73 game because of my contribution to putting that All-Ireland side together. That was a political decision, which quite frankly should never have been allowed. I'm proud of the fact that I sacrificed my career although they never picked me again. There was one repercussion. I had played in the World Cup in '58 and because we created history by getting to the quarter-final they presented us all with a gold watch. Me being an A.D. Dougan, I called my eldest boy A.D. Dougan after me. I gave him the gold watch. I've got another son. I only had another seven caps to go to reach 50 caps and when you play 50 times for Ireland you get a gold watch. I would have given that other gold watch to my youngest son. But that's the way it worked out.

'It's amazing discovering how many people from the North went down to that match. So many people today say to me: "You were right, you were right." But the trouble really is that there are so many vested interests in Dublin and Belfast, either in terms of junkets or free trips. At that time I made a decision to play against the cream. If you're a writer or a journalist working for the local newspaper, your ambition is to write for a national newspaper and so on. I was the same. I just wanted to play against the best in the world. And I did.'

The enigmatic and flamboyant Derek Dougan emerged from working-class East Belfast in the late 1950s. He came from a family rooted in the city's shipyards, with generation after generation earning their living at Harland and Wolff. Although Derek would also spend time at the shipyards as an apprentice electrician, it was football that really caught his attention. As a schoolboy international he showed great promise. Playing for Cregagh Boys, he was soon being courted by Irish League clubs. Distillery won the battle for his signature and he was turning out for their first team by the age of 15.

Predictably, English League clubs came sniffing when they heard of the talents being displayed by the young Derek Dougan. First came Preston North End, whose offer of a contract he rejected. Then came an offer from Portsmouth, which he gladly accepted. It was all happening so quickly. By October 1957 he was making his first-team début against Manchester United's Busby Babes. Soon he was being selected for Northern Ireland senior squads. The timing was perfect. He made his senior international début against Czechoslovakia in 1958. Nothing unusual about that, you might say, except this was in the World Cup finals in Halmstad, Sweden.

'I played in the first match, against Czechoslovakia, and we won 1–0,' Derek says. 'It is standard policy that you never change a winning side. But, to my horror and my unbelievable surprise, they played a guy called Fay Coyle in the next match. And they were beaten 3–1 by Argentina. I thought: "Well, I'll be brought back for the West German game." But I never played again. Peter Doherty, the manager, took me to one side and said: "You're young, you've a great future ahead of you." But I just couldn't believe it. I'm still gob-smacked. It was a load of nonsense. I could have played centre-half. I was a better centre-half than the ones they played. I was a better player than anybody on the Irish team at that time. And I just couldn't believe that I was restricted to one match.'

You would expect a player with a 100 per cent success record in a World Cup finals to have collected a winner's medal. Unfortunately, after his single victorious appearance in Sweden, Derek Dougan had no such luck. As it happened, Northern Ireland dropped out of the tournament, having reached the quarter-finals, and it would take some time before Derek would secure his second cap. Soon he joined Blackburn Rovers, where he put in a losing appearance in the 1960 FA Cup final against Wolves. Thereafter followed a succession of moves, first to Aston Villa, then to Peterborough, next to Leicester City and finally to Wolverhampton Wanderers. He signed for Wolves in March 1967. Throughout all that time he was scoring an abundance of goals, consistently hitting the net in League and Cup matches while gaining a reputation for his heading ability and his speed off the mark.

'I developed a technique in the air that no other centre-forward in history was able to develop,' Derek remarks. 'My timing was unique. But what I had to back me up was this amazing speed. People didn't realise how fast I was until I'd join a club. I used to give Ally McLeod, at Blackburn Rovers, six yards of a start. He'd be on the six-yard box and I'd be on the touchline and I'd race him to the 18-yards and I'd beat him over 18 yards.

'I had a great ability on the ground. Unfortunately that ability was never really fulfilled to its potential for no other reason than when you're playing centre-forward a lot of balls are coming in up in the air and they're going down the flanks to you. There's not a lot you can do. I was just able to develop the ability that if I had one chance I scored. If I had three chances I may get two. You get some guys who if they get five or six chances they may just pop one in the back of the net.

'I also had this unique record that everybody who played up front with me scored goals. I regret not really having a selfish, jealous streak in myself. People used to think I was an individual; that I went out there as a solo performer and I just wanted to entertain the crowd. I did that but I was a better team player than people gave me credit for. I also was so blessed that I played with probably the most gifted outside-left in English football, certainly in my time. He was a guy called David Wagstaffe. I would tell David from set pieces or from corner-kicks where to put it. I said: "David, don't bother about my position, just put it there and I'll find it." And that was 95 per cent successful.'

There was no denying the magnificent history of Wolverhampton Wanderers that overshadowed the club at the time of Derek's arrival. Great names like Billy Wright and Stan Cullis were accorded legendary status. Championship successes in 1954, 1958 and 1959 were fondly recalled. The FA Cup was won in 1960. Unfortunately, as the 1960s progressed the club's fortunes faltered. In 1965 they were relegated. By 1967, at the time of Derek's arrival, they were still in the Second Division. However, all that would soon change. Promotion in 1967 was followed by a period of consolidation. Then in the 1970s came a burst of success. And central to it all was Derek Dougan, a player who netted a hat-trick on his home début against Hull City and who became Wolves' top marksman in the 1967–68, 1968–69 and 1971–72 seasons.

The 1970s also brought wonderful European contests to Molineux, with exotic teams like Juventus (against whom Derek scored), Carl Zeiss Jena, Ferencvaros, F.C. Porto and F.C. Den Haag arriving to do battle in the UEFA Cup. Derek netted a hat-trick against the Portuguese side Académica Coimbra in the UEFA Cup in 1971–72, which was his second hat-trick in five days. He also did battle against Tottenham Hotspur in the final of the UEFA Cup in 1972, which Wolves narrowly lost. Throughout those campaigns Derek became Wolves' top-scorer in European competitions and he also set up a devastating partnership with another Wolves' striker, John Richards. Whether in FA Cup matches, League Championships, League Cups or European campaigns, the Dougan–Richards partnership was feared and respected.

'Probably the Dougan–Richards partnership was the most successful in post-war years, in terms of the number of goals we scored over a four-year period,' Derek claims. 'The reason why it was so successful was because Richards had tremendous speed as well. And he was powerful. In the second season alone we scored well over 50 goals. It was unique. It's really that I was able to make a lot of goals. There was the favourite trick I had of going down the line and cutting it back for guys. And that again was just because of speed.'

It took until 1974 for Derek Dougan and Wolverhampton Wanderers to secure a major trophy success. The prize was the League Cup, which was contested between Wolves and Manchester City at Wembley Stadium. City had a star-studded side with players like Mike Summerbee, Francis Lee, Colin Bell, Denis Law and Rodney Marsh. Wolves had their own stars in Derek Dougan, John Richards, Dave Wagstaffe, Mike Bailey and Alan Sunderland. It was a great day for Wolverhampton Wanderers, who won 2–1. The City players magnanimously applauded Wolves as they walked down from the Royal Box. The gesture was appropriate as this, after all, was Wolves' first major trophy in 14 years.

'Fourteen years earlier I played for Blackburn Rovers against Wolverhampton Wanderers in the 1960 FA Cup final,' Derek remarks. 'Quite frankly, that's one of the things I have regretted in my life. I should never have played. I pulled a muscle the week before. I was on such good form. I had scored both goals in the semi-final. I thought: "I'll be able to get through this and they'll be able to assist me." But I regret playing in that match. If I had been a fit guy I sometimes dream about how it would have turned out.

'Then 14 years later I go back to Wembley playing for Wolverhampton Wanderers Football Club against what at that particular time was maybe the best team in the country and that was Manchester City. And we beat them. The best team won on that particular day. It was unique because for Wolverhampton Wanderers that was the first time in their history they had won the League Cup. I was dead chuffed about that because I fall into the category of a lot of footballers that never won either the FA Cup or a Championship medal. Gordon Banks was another. It's just how it works out. I think about some guys that have actually won Championship medals and were just second-rate footballers. It happens.'

Following his solitary appearance for Northern Ireland in the

1958 World Cup, Derek Dougan went on to win a total of 43 caps for the international side. Right up to 1973 he continued to appear in Northern Ireland colours, playing against the home countries and national teams from the likes of Italy, Spain, Turkey, USSR and West Germany. They weren't particularly impressive years in the province's history. However, the team did contain some remarkable players including George Best, Pat Jennings, Pat Rice, Sammy Nelson, Allan Hunter and Eric McMordie, not to mention Derek Dougan himself. From Derek's earlier era, in the late 1950s, came another galaxy of stars including Danny Blanchflower, Billy Bingham, Harry Gregg, Jimmy McIlroy, Wilbur Cush, Peter McParland, Alf McMichael, Dick Keith and Willie Cunningham. Between them, the two squads contained a mighty collection of football talent.

'I was involved for 15 years,' Derek reflects. 'Having played with and been involved with that old squad – Bingham, Blanchflower, McIlroy, Gregg, Willie Cunningham, Alf McMichael, Dick Keith – I'm often asked: "Which is the better side?" The side I played in from '65 was certainly a better squad. McIlroy would have got in the side. Bingham would have got into the side. Certainly Wilbur could have got in the side. But there would only be about four. Peter McParland might have been a powerful ally for me playing in the side. And everyone else would have been from the '65 to '73 squad.

'Harry Gregg was not in the same league as Pat Jennings. You had Nelson and Pat Rice but Alex Elder was a far better left-back than Sammy Nelson. Liam O'Kane was a good centre-half but a better centre-half than him was big Allan Hunter. He was a powerful centre-half. Eric McMordie was a very talented inside-forward and a wee tough cookie as well, a smashing wee fellow. If I could blend those two squads together, what a side we'd have! We'd give anybody a run for their money. Who do you pick in those teams?

'You would have a backbone down your side – a good goalie Pat Jennings, a good centre-half Allan Hunter, myself at centre-forward and that wee man Best outside who was simply magical on the ball, without a doubt the best footballer I've ever seen. But when you think about it it's a crying shame that two of the best footballers over the last 100 years, and possibly the best footballer of all time, both Irish, never played in the World Cup. That's Liam Brady and George Best. What a shame.'

By the mid-1970s Derek Dougan was in the twilight of his career and his days at Wolves were numbered. Well into his 30s and plagued by back problems, in 1975 he finally decided to quit. He had, by then, not only faithfully served the Wolverhampton club for more than eight seasons but he had also performed with distinction as chairman of the Professional Footballers' Association. His time on the football pitch, however, was over. The powerhouse who had scored 123 goals for Wolves, including five hat-tricks, was about to hang up his boots. The partnership with John Richards that had lit up the football stage in the first half of the 1970s was finished.

For fans of Wolverhampton Wanderers it was clear that one of the club's great eras had come to an end. With the departure of the 43-times capped Northern Ireland international, the steam seemed to go out of the Wolves' revival. The European battles, the Cup runs and the sparkling Championship campaigns all seemed to fizzle out. It came as no surprise in 1976 when the club were relegated to the old Second Division. By then, however, the player affectionately referred to as 'Doog' had departed the stage, wrapping up his career as a substitute in a home match against Leeds United in April 1975.

'By the time that I reached 37 I had another year of my contract to go,' Derek concludes. 'I had reached the stage where a lot of things off the field were going very well for me. But my wife was the only one that actually knew the serious problems I had with my back. Three different surgeons told me that my back problem was a continual muscular spasm. I knew it was more serious than that. So I decided in '75 that I should just retire, purely and simply because it was restricting me. It was restricting me in getting out of bed in the morning. It was restricting me a little bit in training. It was restricting me when I was playing. I eventually had an operation but I deeply regret not having that operation in '75 because there is no doubt in my own mind that I would have played on for a number of years after that, to what level would be the question mark.

'But having gone through it and having played for the best part of 25 years, when you consider the average life of a footballer is only eight years then I had really three lives instead of one. I played until I was 37. And, by the way, I still scored goals in Europe and the First Division at 37. I'm quite proud of that fact. It's like us all; we would like to go on forever but you've got to be realistic and know that you can't. The only slight jealousy that I've got is not that I'm envious about the dough the guys are earning today. The only thing I'm envious about is the state of the football grounds today. They are absolutely fantastic.

'I look back at it and think: "My God, somebody paid me to train every day, be healthy, be fit, go and entertain people, hopefully excite people, hopefully score a few goals, read about yourself on a Sunday, see yourself on *Match of the Day*, hear about something you've said on the radio or somebody describing you." That really is probably the perfect life. The only people that could possibly better that would probably be film stars and people who are seriously in the public way. You're always remembered for your contribution and people still recognise me and still say hello. I'm very lucky.

'When I look back, I've been to four-fifths of the world. I have captained my country. I have played for six very good clubs. I've scored so many goals it just isn't true. Sometimes I've got to pinch myself when I think of some of the goals I've scored and the countries I've been to. It is just absolutely monumental. And, of course, I'm like all footballers. We are just like the Chelsea pensioners – we don't die, we just fade away. So, yeah, the 25 years, which was three careers in one, it's all been worthwhile. And I'm delighted I'm still here to tell the tale.'

9. DON GIVENS

OCTOBER IS A POPULAR MONTH WITH DON GIVENS. IN OCTOBER 1974 HE SCORED THREE goals against the mighty Soviet Union. Twelve months later, in October 1975, he hammered four past the hapless Turks. As if that weren't enough, he also chalked up huge tallies in League matches surrounding both those games. He scored three League goals for Queen's Park Rangers in the week of the Soviet match and two in the week of the match against Turkey, bringing his grand total for each of those weeks to six. There must have been something in the October air that inspired Don Givens.

It wasn't as if the matches were exhibition games, either. In October 1974 some 35,000 spectators witnessed the European Championship qualifier against the Soviet Union at Dalymount Park. It was Liam Brady's first game for his country. The wonderful Oleg Blokhin played for the visitors. A place in the European Championship finals was at stake. Although hopes of qualification were high, by the time the match against Turkey came around the following year those hopes had been dashed. For Don Givens, however, there was some consolation. His four-goal tally against Turkey equalled Paddy Moore's record set against Belgium back in 1934. Remarkably, three of those goals were scored in nine minutes. Those matches also set Don on the road to 19 international goals, which was a record that lasted for a decade.

'I remember the goals all right,' Don says of his hat-trick against the Soviet Union. 'I haven't forgotten the goals because an awful lot of people seem to have been at Dalymount that day. Everybody I've met since was at the game and they always remind me. But when I look back on it I think the performance was excellent. I think it was Liam Brady's first game and Liam had hair down to his shoulders. He was only 18 and he looked like he'd been in the international team for 10 years. But what I didn't realise until I'd seen a tape of the game was the amount of good football we played that day.

'I thought the first goal was probably one of the better goals that I scored. I think Johnny Giles hit a pass to Joe Kinnear out wide. Joe got to about 25 yards out and he knocked a cross in. There was a lot of pace to the cross. I think it was probably outside the penalty spot. I sort of glanced it into the bottom corner and that set us off.

'The second one came from a long throw-in from Steve Heighway, which was something we used now and again. The ball bobbled about. I think Ray Treacy might have touched it on and then I hooked it in from close range. I didn't realise it at the time but I would say looking back that I might possibly have been offside when I stuck it in.

'The third one was a free kick out wide from Johnny Giles in the second half. It was something that we worked on in training. As soon as John put his hand on the ball, as soon as I made the run, he'd pop it into the near-post spot, which he did, and I glanced it in. It was a great day all round.

'In that match against the Soviet Union I scored three on the Wednesday, I had scored two with QPR the previous Saturday and when I went back to QPR I scored another one. So it was six in that week. In exactly the same week a year later I scored one on the Saturday, four against Turkey on the Wednesday and one again on the Saturday. October obviously was a good time for me in those days. It is strange when I look back at those weeks in '74 and '75. Six goals in a week each time was incredible.'

A young Don Givens arrived at Manchester United in 1966 right at the heart of one of the club's greatest eras. Following an FA Cup victory in 1963 and a League Championship in 1964–65, United had already embarked on one of the finest periods in their history. With a further League Championship in 1966–67 and the European Cup in 1968, United became one of the most fashionable and successful clubs in European football. Their team was crammed with stars like Best, Law and Charlton. And into that hotbed of history, tradition, ambition and talent stepped Don Givens, aged 17, who also happened to be a fan of the Reds.

Those 1960s' years were heady years indeed for this young boy just over from Dublin. Although overawed by the glamour of Manchester United's great stars, Don eventually worked his way into the first team and made his début as a substitute replacement for Tony Dunne in a 2–2 away draw at Crystal Palace. Following that introduction to First Division football in August 1969, he went on to make nine appearances for the club and scored one goal in a 3–1 home victory over Sunderland. Although largely forgotten as a Manchester United player, it was at Old Trafford that Don Givens first honed his skills.

'It was a great time to be there,' Don recalls of his time with Manchester United. 'I got the chance to go to United for a trial and was taken on as an apprentice, as it was in those days. I was a United fan, so it was like a dream to be mixing with players like Best, Charlton, Law and Stiles. They were idols of mine. It was a great adventure. It was a little bit tough at the time to make a breakthrough in that kind of company, although I ended up having about eight or nine games in the first team on odd occasions when maybe Denis Law was injured.

'The first time I ever got on the team was down at Crystal Palace in the first game of the season. I was sub and it was a time when there was only one sub. Subs had only recently been introduced. Tony Dunne got injured with about 10 minutes to go. I went on and played right-back for 10 minutes. A few games later we went to Everton, to Goodison Park, and I was picked to play in midfield, which was strange when I look back now because I was basically a centre-forward. Everton had a good team with Alan Ball and Harvey and Kendall, and we lost there. That was the season when I had some odd appearances in the first team, but when the season was over I was put on the list.

'At the end of the season the first team were going to America on tour and, having had some games in the first team, I thought that I might be in with a shout of going with them. We were jogging around the training-ground and people were getting pulled and told to go up and see the boss. Stupid as it might seem now, I thought I was about to be measured up for the blazer to go to America. That's when he said to me: "You're gone." It was heartbreaking at the time because I was a United supporter. It was a real blow. But when I look back I think it was probably the best thing that ever happened to me.

'I went to a Second Division club, which was Luton. They bought me for £15,000. But the fact that I was bought as a first-team player made a big difference to my confidence. Suddenly I was a first-team player, albeit in the Second Division. From there I went on to QPR and, looking back, Manchester United did me a favour really rather than letting me hang around for another year or two.

'QPR were a very nice team to play in. When I first joined, Gordon Jago was manager. Very soon after that, Dave Sexton took over. Dave was a very good coach and had a very good knowledge of the game. He was the first manager I remember in England who went to other European countries to learn things. Dave used to go and watch Mönchengladbach when Hennes Weisweiler was the coach and also the great Ajax team with Cruyff. He would go and watch them at the weekend, usually on a Sunday when they played in Germany. Dave would come back Monday morning with something to work on in training.

'From an attacking point of view, QPR were a great team to play in. We had some very good players like Stan Bowles, Gerry Francis, Dave Thomas and Frank McLintock. We had a very good team at the time. With Dave's policy of attacking, it was great to play in the team and things went very well for me for a few years.'

Given his growing status at Manchester United in the late 1960s, it wasn't surprising that Don Givens quickly made his way into the Republic of Ireland international side. He made his first appearance for his country against Denmark in 1969. Although he was soon forced to leave Old Trafford for Luton Town and later Queen's Park Rangers, where he played during the remaining bulk of his career in England, his appearances with the international side continued without interruption.

As a member of Queen's Park Rangers' great team of the mid-1970s, Don produced his most sparkling form for the international side. At the time, QPR were an extraordinarily successful club, finishing in the upper reaches of the old First Division and playing before record attendances at Loftus Road. With players like John Hollins, David Webb, Dave Thomas, Phil Parkes, Gerry Francis, Stan Bowles, Dave Clement and Don Givens, the team was crammed with the finest football talent. Players like Parkes, Francis, Clement and Bowles played for England, Don Masson for Scotland, while Givens made regular forays back to Dublin or throughout Europe with his international colleagues. Luckily for the national side, he could transfer his goal-scoring prowess from club to country with relative ease.

From 1969 through the bulk of the 1970s, Don was a virtual ever-present in the national side, becoming a consistent and prolific goal-scorer throughout most of that era. Those were years when Irish soccer struggled to emerge from the heroic failures of the 1950s and 1960s. The near misses at qualification for the World Cup finals in Sweden in 1958 and England in 1966 would, it was hoped, become a thing of the past. Managers came and went. Mick Meagan gave way to Liam Tuohy and Seán Thomas. Next came Johnny Giles. And with each of those managerial changes came genuine progress in developing a professional set-up that could match the standards being set elsewhere in Europe.

'I think the balance was quite good at the time,' Don says of the international side in the 1970s. 'Before Frank Stapleton came on board, the front three were Ray Treacy and myself and Stevie Heighway out wide. Stevie provided the ammunition and Ray and I seemed to hit it off. Ray was selected sometimes for the international team when he wasn't in his club team, but he worked well with me and it suited the team very well. In the middle of the field, Gerry Daly had emerged at Manchester United, but the balance provided by Mick Martin, Johnny Giles and Liam Brady worked well. Then we had Jimmy Holmes and Joe Kinnear. Paddy Mulligan was there as well. In the Soviet Union game it was Terry Mancini but sometimes it was Eoin Hand. In some ways the team picked itself and we got very used to each other.

'It was a different era. Nowadays, we have a depth in the squad and through the U-21s there's some decent players coming through. It was much more difficult in those times. The manager didn't always pick the squad; a committee picked it and then he was given the squad. We weren't very well organised in those early days. But when Liam Tuohy and then Johnny Giles took over, things moved on a little bit from there and we became a bit more professional. Probably because of the limited selection, we had a fairly settled team, which helped a little bit. When you played for Ireland you knew the players very well. We started to get to know each other a little better because of that.

'Over the years other players started to come through. There was Frank Stapleton and Dave O'Leary. Tony Grealish and others started to make inroads. Suddenly, I felt that a bit more depth came into the thing and it just continued on. There was a great group of players and a great camaraderie. I still speak to Terry Conroy, Mick Martin, Jimmy Holmes and Johnny Giles and there's still an element of togetherness there that might not be there 20 years on with this present team. In those days we had great fun. We had great sing-songs after the game. It was easier to get a ticket for the match than to get into the sing-songs, which were organised by Johnny Giles and Ray Treacy. We had people like Paddy Reilly and the Dublin City Ramblers and Luke Kelly, God rest his soul, who would be there as well. So it was great. There was a great atmosphere about the place.

'We were very, very unlucky. The last campaign I was involved in we got beaten on goal difference and failed to qualify for the '82 World Cup. France went instead of us on goal difference. We were always in tough groups because up until then we had never done anything to merit any kind of seeding. We were always the rubbish thrown in at the end of the grouping with the Leichtensteins. At the time we weren't much better than them. Certainly the results didn't show it. Now things have changed a little bit. The qualifications with Jack Charlton lifted our standing up a long way in international football and consequently we get in easier groups. But it was very tough in those days to be drawn with three or four very decent teams in a group, especially with us not having a very professional approach. The nearest we came, from my point of view anyway, was in '82.

'I think we needed a little bit of luck. When I first started playing with the international team we weren't very well organised and I don't think we deserved any luck because of the way things were run. Then as we got more professional the luck didn't come with us. When I look back at Jack's first qualification, there was a stroke of luck in that, in the match in Bulgaria when Scotland scored, and that set us on the way to Germany. That little bit of luck we didn't have. I think certainly around the end of the 1970s and early 1980s we weren't very far away from qualification and that bit of luck might have just tipped the balance our way.'

From the time he scored his first international goal against

Hungary in June 1969, the floodgates seemed to open for Don Givens. He hammered in goals against Scotland and Denmark. He scored against Poland and Iran. He chalked up those massive tallies against the Soviet Union and Turkey. He beat keepers from Bulgaria, Switzerland and the USA. In fact, throughout the 1970s nobody could quite match the scoring feats of Don Givens. Gradually he edged up the scoring tables. By the time he had quit he held the record of 19 international goals, which was a record that would stand for a decade.

'I don't think scoring goals is an art,' Don remarks. 'If you're a forward it's your job. Your job doesn't end there. I never felt that I was a real goal-poacher. I felt that I should work across the line and help the team and make moves for other people. But at the end of the day if you're a centre-forward come the end of the season somebody is going to say: "How many did you score?" because that's what your job is. I suppose it's like anybody working in industry; you have to account for what you do. As a centre-forward you go through bad times but over a season, if you have the ability and you have the hunger, you'll get your share of goals as long as you can play a bit. That was the thing for me. If I was a centre-forward I wanted to say that I've scored so many goals per season. It doesn't always work out like that but that was the aim.

'The record was a source of pride. It carried on for a lot longer than I expected because in the early days we didn't play as many matches. I ended up with my record being 19 goals from 56 games. There was a period when John Aldridge and Frank Stapleton and Niall Quinn had much more games, but maybe the pressure was more on them. Certainly it was a great source of pride for me to have that record for such a long time. I always wanted the boys to score, but maybe somebody else on the team other than John or Frank or Niall because I would like to have been remembered for that. However, like any record, it gets broken in the end.'

Following his productive years with Queen's Park Rangers, Don Givens transferred his goal-scoring skills first to Birmingham City and then to Bournemouth and Sheffield United. Then in 1981 he made what was at the time an unusual and surprising move to Swiss club, Neuchâtel Xamax. In those days not a lot was known about football in Switzerland and Neuchâtel Xamax were little regarded in

European football circles. All that would soon change, however, as Don Givens continued to score prolifically while helping the club to unprecedented success in Europe. He also captained them to a Swiss League Championship and eventually coached them following his retirement as a player. Even today, Don Givens is recalled by Neuchâtel Xamax' fans with the reverence afforded only to legends.

'While I was at Sheffield United, Harry Haslam, who had originally taken me from Manchester United to Luton, asked me what I was going to do,' Don says regarding his move to Swiss football. 'I said I was kind of thinking about going abroad. He had a contact in Switzerland and that's really how it came about.

'I went over with Harry to see Neuchâtel, whom I had never heard of at the time. I had heard of Young Boys and Grasshoppers and I had heard of Servette but I had never heard of Neuchâtel. I saw them play their last game and they won that game and qualified for the UEFA Cup for the first time in their history. They were basically a small-town team that had built up. So I joined them and the first season we were in the UEFA Cup.

'We had a marvellous run in the UEFA Cup the first season I joined them. We got to the quarter-finals, which was incredible for a Swiss team, and that really got the town buzzing. I had six seasons playing there in Neuchâtel and it was absolutely marvellous. The whole thing was rolling along. Eventually we won the title in my last season, when I was captain, and it was a kind of fairy-tale ending to my career.'

As a striker, Don Givens had all the predatory instincts necessary for survival at the highest level of the game. He could head the ball with power and accuracy but he could also use his feet to devastating effect. Although an instinctive goal-scorer, he was unselfish in his play and was known as a striker who always passed to colleagues who were better placed to score. After leaving football he applied his technical knowledge as a youth coach with Arsenal. Later he coached the Republic of Ireland U-21s and even stepped in as temporary senior manager following the retirement of Mick McCarthy as national coach.

With QPR, Don was part of one of the finest football sides ever to grace the English game. For one brief spell, Dave Sexton's team threatened to sweep all before them in the First Division, producing a brand of fluid, attacking, total football rarely seen in Britain. Playing at centre-forward, Don came close in 1975–76 to winning a League Championship medal only to be narrowly beaten to the title by Liverpool. Tragically, that elusive League medal slipped away in the closing match of the season when Liverpool came from behind to secure the win they needed to become League champions. QPR had to settle for second place.

For Irish fans, however, the memory of Don Givens will always be linked to his appearances in the green shirt of his country, particularly in those historic matches against the Soviet Union and Turkey in 1974 and 1975 respectively. For those who saw him play at venues like Dalymount Park or Lansdowne Road, Don faithfully reproduced the scoring talents he displayed in domestic League matches or in FA Cup competitions. That he could straddle the divide between club and international football with such ease was in itself remarkable. That he did so while becoming the Republic's record scorer for a full decade was perhaps his ultimate triumph in the game of football.

'My biggest memory of the international team would be when I used to go to Dalymount usually on a Sunday afternoon to watch Noel Cantwell and Charlie Hurley and people like that,' Don concludes. 'The thing that always stuck in my mind was the players standing for the national anthem. When that happened to me during my first game at home against Hungary, when I was now standing in that line for the national anthem, it was probably the biggest thing that I'll remember. It's what separates international football from club football. I've played in important League matches and Cup matches and they mean a lot. But nothing means half as much as standing when the national anthem is playing and you realise you are playing for your country. I think that's something I'll never forget.'

10. FRANK STAPLETON

THERE WAS AN AURA OF DANGER SURROUNDING STRIKER FRANK STAPLETON. HE HAD A towering presence in the penalty box. His strength and aggression were fearsome. His power with headers was respected far and wide. His sense of position was exceptional. Not surprisingly he scored 108 goals for Arsenal. He added a further 78 at Manchester United, both tallies being achieved at the highest level of the game in the competitive 1970s and 1980s. He once held the record for the Republic of Ireland of 20 goals, which lasted for over a decade. Few strikers at any level of football could lay claim to a nose for goal deadlier than Frank Stapleton's.

'I think that's what Arsenal noticed at the start,' Frank says of his shooting prowess. 'I was big and strong and I used to get my fair share of goals. But when you go to a professional club you're talking about a different game altogether. It's a different level. You have to have more of an all-round game. You have to have speed. You have to have strength. You've got to have ability. You've got to have control of the ball. Those skills have to be better than they were when you were playing schoolboy football. Those two or three years when you are trying to make your way in the game are your learning process.

'A lot of players don't reach the standard. Say there are five qualifications. They may only reach four and that's not good enough. You have to be good at five things. I had the strength that I could head the ball and score goals. But I had to work very hard at my control and passing and things like that. Through hard work it came about. You don't obviously just walk out onto a football pitch. You might have ability but if you don't work at it, it doesn't mean anything. You have to really work your socks off and then there's no guarantee that it will happen for you either.

'I joined a big club at Arsenal and then I went to Manchester United. A lot of players can't cope with what's expected, with the need for performance levels to be high all the time. It's very hard to put your finger on it. Manchester United have bought big in years gone by, where they've paid a lot of money for players and they can't cope with the pressure that exists at a big club. They also look for entertainment value at Old Trafford. It just has to be in you, you have to be able to react and that's down to temperament. You see players with great ability and they freeze in those situations. It's very easy to buckle and it's quite understandable that people wouldn't be able to cope with that sort of pressure. But I was fortunate that I was able to deal with it.'

There was one remarkable period in the 1970s and 1980s when it seemed that the Irish owned Arsenal. From the Republic of Ireland came Frank Stapleton, Liam Brady, David O'Leary and John Devine. From Northern Ireland came Pat Jennings, Pat Rice and Sammy Nelson. All of them played at international level. They each were stars in their own right. Reinforcing the association, the Arsenal manager Terry Neill also was from Northern Ireland. No other member of the Irish contingent, however, showed quite the same appetite for rattling the net as Frank Stapleton.

'The club treated me very well when I came over,' Frank recalls of his trial at Arsenal in 1972. 'I only went for a weekend and they were very good with me. The chief scout said: "Look, we'd like to sign you but I want to come over and speak to your parents, answer any questions they've got." It was that personal touch. The middle of the following week, the chief scout Gordon Clark came over and said to my parents: "Right, this is what we want with him." My mother asked most of the questions. My dad said: "Well, it's your decision, you've got to go and live there and you've got to live with that decision. It would be my choice but you shouldn't let that influence you."

'The first year was very hard. You're in digs and they put you with a family. It takes time. I think at that time there was more of a cultural difference than there is now. Travel is easier now. But certainly the first year was very hard coming to terms with London. The difficult thing as well was the training, the sort of regime you were under. You were living with a family in digs in London and if you stepped out of line they were on to the club. So you were disciplined outside of football but also within football as well. It was a very disciplined game.'

From his breakthrough in 1975, Frank Stapleton shone in the Arsenal attack. Lift-off was slow, with the team hovering initially in the lower half of the table. For the last four seasons of the 1970s, however, the club climbed to top-half respectability in the First Division. In the FA Cup the story was considerably better. In 1978 they reached the final only to be beaten by Ipswich Town. The following year they won the trophy in a cracking game against Manchester United. In the 1980 final they lost to West Ham. They also reached the final of the European Cup Winners' Cup in 1980, losing to Valencia on penalties. Throughout those years Frank chalked up a remarkable scoring tally, hammering home 108 goals in his appearances for the club up to his departure in 1981.

'We were always a bit short in terms of the squad,' Frank remarks. 'We were always three players short. But the club was run very tightly and they didn't splash money out. We produced good players but whenever they bought anybody it was always at the expense of somebody going out. Look at the top clubs today; they have massive squads. I know there's a lot more money in the game now and that's significant. But at Arsenal, for the stature that the club had at the time I just felt they needed to be a bit more ambitious. And I don't think they were.

'That was unfortunate. We were all coming in after the Double in 1971. They did fantastically well to win the Double but those players all aged and then there was a new bunch of players coming through. I wonder what would Arsenal have done if they hadn't brought that bunch of fellows through? They would have to have gone out to buy people. And if they were that restricted with their money they might have to have bought a lot of mediocre players. But I think we were still three players short and that was a big disappointment although we went close on a couple of occasions.

'The reason we had such a good Cup run was because we could always cope with those situations. We could get over the difficult hurdles early on and then it just seemed to roll from there. In the Cup if you get to the next round it comes two to three weeks after you've played your initial third-round tie, and then on from there.

Every time it comes around you can build yourself up for one match. But with the League it's a marathon, it's sustained over a long time. The League is a bit more about consistency. And obviously you haven't enough players to get you through a season when you get injuries or loss of form.'

Of the three-in-a-row FA Cup final appearances, the one to stick in Arsenal fans' memories was the victory in 1979. That was an extraordinary match, with an explosive finish. Arsenal's two-goal lead was negated by a brace from Manchester United in the game's closing minutes. With extra time imminent, Liam Brady started the move that saw Alan Sunderland score. For those at Wembley or watching at home, the final whistle, which came seconds later, was a welcome relief from the tension. For the record, Arsenal won 3–2 with one of their goals scored by Frank Stapleton.

'It was such a significant Cup final,' Frank says. 'It's a little bit numbing at the time. You have one end of the ground that's quiet. In the other end everybody is ecstatic. It tended to pass you by. The real enjoyment came when the season had finished and you settled down. You were maybe going for a holiday and you could sit back and really enjoy the day better. It's like a dream. You just kind of wake up and the reality hits you. That's what it was like at that particular time.

'One of the highlights of your playing career is obviously when you score goals. But the fact that you score in such a game, in a Cup final that is going out worldwide, I think that was extra satisfying. It was the first time we'd won anything as a team. Liam dribbled through, passed about four players, it was on his right foot and I wasn't sure that he was going to get it across. But on the day he was mesmerising. I just made sure that I made good contact with the ball. A lot of people said it was an easy goal but it was very easy from there to put it over the bar or give the goalkeeper a chance. I think the thing about the goal was more Liam's run than me putting it in the net.'

It took until October 1976 for Frank Stapleton to win his first cap for the Republic of Ireland. Under the managerial guidance of Johnny Giles, the team travelled to Turkey for a friendly in the build-up to the World Cup qualifier scheduled for later in the year. Places were up for grabs. The team was beginning to take shape, featuring high-calibre players like Liam Brady, Don Givens, Mick Martin, Paddy Mulligan, Gerry Daly and Terry Conroy. Not to be outshone, the new kid on the block Frank Stapleton got off to a blistering start with a score just three minutes into the game. After that performance, he was an automatic choice on the international side.

'I had been in the squad a couple of times and then I travelled to Turkey,' Frank recalls. 'It's always a game where a lot of players think: "I don't fancy that long trip." In those days we didn't have charter flights, we had to travel through Zürich. We had to meet in London first. A lot of lads met in London on the Sunday. It would obviously take you a couple of days to get over it. But we went out there and I scored after three minutes. We drew the game 3–3. To get your first cap and score a goal as well was fantastic. The only disappointment was that it wasn't in Dublin, in front of your own supporters.

'We got a free and I used to have this routine with Liam. I used to run away with my back to him and not look like I was interested. It was just a natural thing. But Johnny Giles took the free and he screamed at me. I knew where the ball was going to go. I got a header to it and it went in the bottom corner. I was walking away and Johnny Giles had a right go. He said: "Bloody hell, wake up." I said: "I wasn't asleep." Liam came over and said: "What are you doing? He's just scored a goal and you're having a go at him!" It was comical really. I think Johnny thought I was asleep. But it was just this thing that if you don't look interested defenders think: "Well, wait until he gets into position." Then you go for the space. It worked out and it was a fantastic feeling.

'Johnny Giles was the manager and he was looking to improve things all the time. But he was having to battle all the time with the FAI to try and tell them: "Players are expecting more, if you want them to be professional you've got to show a professional attitude towards them and provide everything that will make it easier for them to do the job." It was fairly difficult but it wasn't too bad. The only problem was travelling away from home. We all had to meet somewhere in England and from that point we would all be together. We'd always travel through Zürich. If we were going to Eastern Europe we always travelled through Zürich. It was an extra three or four hours.

'When you played a midweek international match away, you'd get

ROY KEANE
Roy Keane drove Manchester United to Doubles, a famous Treble and propelled them to European success.

PAUL McGRATH
Paul McGrath played 83 times for his country despite problems with his 'dodgy knees'.

DAVID O'LEARY
A jubilant David O'Leary after scoring the winning penalty in the shootout with Romania at Italia '90.

ALAN KELLY
Goalkeeper Alan Kelly played for the Republic of Ireland from 1956 to 1973.

DEREK DOUGAN
Northern Ireland striker Derek Dougan played with victorious
Wolves in the 1974 League Cup final at Wembley Stadium.

FRANK STAPLETON
Frank Stapleton scored 20 goals for the Republic of Ireland — a record that lasted for over a decade.

DON GIVENS
Don Givens amassed a one-time Republic of Ireland record of 19 goals.

NOEL CANTWELL
Manchester United captain Noel Cantwell with the FA Cup after his team's victory over Leicester City in 1963.

PACKIE BONNER
Packie Bonner made this famous save in the penalty shootout against Romania at Italia '90.

RONNIE WHELAN
Ronnie Whelan celebrates after scoring against the Soviet Union in the 1988 European Championship finals.

GEORGE BEST
Manchester United's George Best pictured with team-mates Nobby Stiles and Bobby Charlton.

CON MARTIN
Con Martin played for Aston Villa and was capped by both Northern Ireland and the Republic of Ireland.

JOHNNY GILES
Midfield general Johnny Giles starred for Leeds United during the club's golden era in the late 1960s and early 1970s.

PAT JENNINGS

Legendary goalkeeper Pat Jennings won 119 caps for Northern Ireland before retiring at the age of 41.

LIAM BRADY

Playmaker Liam Brady experienced FA Cup success with Arsenal and won two scudetti with Juventus.

NORMAN WHITESIDE
Norman Whiteside (right) lines out for Northern Ireland alongside
Nigel Worthington, Mal Donaghy and Sammy McIlroy.

JACKIE CAREY
Jackie Carey (front row, third from left) pictured with the
Republic of Ireland team that defeated England at Goodison Park in 1949.

NIALL QUINN
Niall Quinn set a new scoring record for the Republic of Ireland at the age of 35.

TONY DUNNE
Tony Dunne (back row, second from left) won two League Championships, the FA Cup and European Cup with Manchester United in the 1960s.

back to the hotel after the game and you'd have something to eat. You'd just go to bed and you'd be up at the crack of dawn. Trying to recover from the match itself is hard enough but we had to travel through the day only having a few hours' sleep. These days the managers want the players back the next day. They look over them, maybe get masseurs in and do all the bits to make sure they don't have any reaction for the next Saturday.

'We used to come back from international games and just hope on the Saturday that the team won. Otherwise the manager would be going mad saying: "You're going away on an international trip yet every time you come back we lose." You were playing on the Saturday from memory because you were so sore and stiff not only from travelling but from the games themselves. The level is a bit higher when you're playing at international level rather than club level. You're playing against the best players from that country and they are *all* better as well.'

In a welter of speculation and complex transfer negotiations, Frank Stapleton left Arsenal for Manchester United in August 1981. He almost signed for Liverpool but was captured instead by Ron Atkinson, who was in the process of enhancing his squad at Old Trafford. Frank went straight into the first team. Those were remarkable years in the history of Manchester United. They never dropped outside the top four in the next five seasons. Unfortunately, in each of those seasons they were beaten to the title by teams from Merseyside: four times by Liverpool and once by Everton. There was some consolation in two FA Cup victories in 1983 and 1985. However, for a club of United's size and ambitions it wasn't enough. Despite Frank's 78 goals, it would take a bit longer for the glory years to return to Old Trafford.

'The club had not won the Championship since 1967,' Frank remarks. 'Obviously, as the years went on, the more pressure came on. In my time we really should have won it twice. We had great runs and we fell away. You put that down to experience. But we really should have won it because of the quality of players that we had on the team. Norman Whiteside came through at the end of my first season there. Bryan Robson was there. Ray Wilkins was there. Arnold Muhren was there. We had wonderful players, as good as anything else in the country, but we just didn't have that consistency.

'We were a decent Cup side. We won the Cup on two occasions but the League evaded us. We really should have won it on two occasions. We were in a good position coming out of Easter one year and we ended up fourth. That is a huge disappointment because we knew we had the team to do it. There were enough players. That was a big disappointment for everybody concerned.'

Of the two FA Cup victories with Manchester United, the one that sticks in Frank's memory is the 1983 victory over Brighton. A thrilling first match ended in a 2–2 draw. Frank scored one of the goals. Brighton showed remarkable resilience. It took a spectacular stop by Gary Bailey in extra time to save Manchester United. However, the replay five days later was a different affair. 'The replay was a foregone conclusion,' Frank says. 'The lads were completely focused on the game and the people who hadn't had a good game on the Saturday all came through. We coasted the match. But that's the history of the FA Cup. It's got so many twists and turns in it.'

On the international front, Frank Stapleton enhanced his reputation in the 1980s with a steady stream of goals for the national side. In the first half of the decade he scored against Cyprus, Czechoslovakia, Holland, France, Iceland, Spain and Malta. He also became a central figure in one of the most talented sides ever to represent the Republic of Ireland. The team in the early 1980s contained top-class players like Liam Brady, David O'Leary, Mark Lawrenson, Michael Robinson, Mick Martin, Kevin Moran, Ronnie Whelan, Gerry Daly, Ashley Grimes and Chris Hughton. But for a few unfortunate results, they could have – and probably should have – become the first Republic of Ireland side to qualify for a World Cup finals.

'When you look at the team coming up to 1982, for many people that is the best team we've had,' Frank says. 'Mark Lawrenson was there, Liam Brady was there, we had Gerry Daly on the team. We had what a lot of people would consider a strong side. But especially when we'd come back after matches, a lot of people would say: "I can't understand how you're not winning games away from home." That was the crux of it.

'Regarding the '82 World Cup we lost out by goal difference, which was a shame. We just missed out to France. I think that year they went through to the semi-final. We had played France in

Dublin, which is one of my most memorable games playing for Ireland. We beat them 3–2. They had Platini, Tigana and all these players playing around that time. They were wonderful players who went on to have wonderful careers. On the day, we really had the crowd behind us. It was one of the classic games at Lansdowne Road. If we had qualified I think that would have taken the team on to even better things. As we saw in subsequent years when we did qualify, the team moved to another level once they had broken the back of qualification. Because we didn't do it, that team is not really remembered. A lot of people wouldn't put the '82 team, or the team around that era, as the best one.'

In the latter half of the 1980s Frank Stapleton continued his goal-scoring feats with the Republic of Ireland, slamming in goals against Switzerland, Denmark, Czechoslovakia, Belgium, Bulgaria, Luxembourg and West Germany. He also captained the side for the European Championship campaign in West Germany, where they famously beat England and drew with the Soviet Union. Although included in Jack Charlton's squad for the 1990 World Cup finals, Frank was rapidly losing favour with his manager and was no longer an automatic choice by the time the team departed for Italy. As a prelude to that campaign he played his final game for his country in the warm-up match against Malta where, on 2 June 1990, he scored his last goal for Ireland.

'Well, I played the previous September against West Germany,' Frank recalls. 'Liam played and Tony Galvin played and Jack took Liam Brady off. I scored that day. I almost scored a second. At the end Jack was very begrudging. He said we did OK. I'd had a good game. I know when I've had a good game. I was on the bench thereafter. I didn't play another game until I got 30 minutes in the Maltese game. I wouldn't have had another cap if they hadn't arranged that game. After we arrived in Malta they decided to have another international friendly and I scored a goal. It was a little bit sour for me because I wasn't being included. I was just there as part of the party. Having been there all the way through and to get to the World Cup and not even get a look-in, that was disappointing.

'At least I went as part of the group. The disappointment was not playing and not being involved. But I enjoyed the victories that we got. To be fair, we didn't get any victories, we got draws and we won in a penalty shootout. But I think the whole fact of us being there, the first time Ireland ever qualified for the World Cup finals, being there and being part of it and seeing the supporters there having a great time and just enjoying the football, that was great. It was a fantastic time. It was a great time for everybody to be involved. Just after the World Cup then I bowed out of international football because I knew I wasn't going to play again.'

To fans of the Republic of Ireland, Frank Stapleton is remembered for his exploits in the national team extending from 1976 to 1990, during which time he accumulated what was for more than a decade a record 20 international goals. To see him visit Old Trafford or Highbury is a remarkable experience. Revered as a legend at both grounds, he is invariably mobbed by Reds and Gunners supporters. Although he went on to play for many other clubs, including Ajax and Le Havre, it's primarily at United and Arsenal that Frank is recalled for his awesome shooting, his powerful headers, his exceptional timing, his devastating goal-scoring ability and his unselfish team play. Few Irish players come even close to matching his contribution to the game of football.

'I had six great years at United,' Frank concludes. 'It's a fantastic club and I've been so lucky. I went to Arsenal first and then I went to Manchester United and they are two of the greatest clubs in Britain. I had a great time and have great memories and got accepted by the supporters. There was never a dissenting word said about me by any of the supporters. Even now, if I go to Old Trafford or Highbury, people have long memories and they are great. I would only ever have good things to say about both clubs.'

11. PAT JENNINGS

THE JOB OF A GOALKEEPER IS A WRETCHED ONE INDEED. YOU'RE ALONE FOR MOST OF the match. When you're not you're being pushed and assaulted by rabid opponents. You can't hide. Make any mistake and the consequences are potentially drastic. If you let in a goal you're roundly abused. You stand in the freezing cold, warming your hands, trying to stay focused. You're the butt-end of jokes and derision from supporters behind your goal. What's more, if you played in the 1970s you feared for your life as lunatics masquerading as fans pummelled your goalmouth with missiles.

Such was the misfortune of Northern Ireland's legendary goalkeeper Pat Jennings. By any standards, his career was a rich one. He was chosen as Footballer of the Year and Players' Player of the Year. He experienced UEFA Cup, FA Cup and League Cup success. He starred in World Cup finals. Yet, above all, while playing at a time when violence was rampant in football, he bore the brunt of some unbelievably vicious physical assaults.

'I've had everything thrown at me from door handles to snooker balls to beer bottles,' Pat recalls of his years in English football. 'They even used coins with the edges sanded down like razor blades. If they had hit you they would have split you and cut you to bits. I played in a game at Everton one afternoon and a Coca-Cola bottle hit me bang on the top of the head. It stunned me for a minute but it didn't knock me out.

'I was playing at Nottingham Forest one afternoon and I went nine or ten yards out of my goal to get a back-pass. Next thing I felt something going into my arm. When I looked down there was a dart stuck full-length into my arm. I pulled it out and went back into the goalmouth and put it in my cap. When I went in at half-time I said to the trainer: "Have a look at my arm, I've had a dart stuck in it." Everybody had a bit of a laugh but Don Howe didn't see the funny side of it. He steamed off into Brian Clough's dressing-room to complain about his players having darts thrown at them. I think they did actually pick up a lad from the crowd and he finished up getting five or six months in jail for it. But it was a scary incident because had it been an eye or something like that it would have been much more serious than an arm.

'There was also one of my very early games with Tottenham during an early part of the season with a very firm pitch. We were 1–0 down against Manchester United. With about two minutes to go, somebody threw the ball from a throw-in to Jimmy Greaves. It was just about the half-way line. Nobby Stiles was marking him and he was shouting and barking to people around him: "Pick up and get tight." Anyway, Jimmy took off and finished up sticking the ball in the net having beaten about six players. That brought it back to 1–1.

'Next thing, I can remember looking down from my goalmouth and seeing Bobby Charlton in full flight, 30 yards from goal, ready to let go of a shot. Beside me were these broken bottles sitting up in the six-yard box. I can still see them vividly. Luckily enough, Alan Mullery came up alongside him and cut across him and got a tackle in. We got the match stopped and got the goalmouth cleared. But I often wonder what would have happened if the shot had come in. Would I have actually dived in this broken glass? Luckily, it didn't come to that. Then Jimmy Greaves picked up another ball and we went on to win the match. Thankfully, all that side of it is gone now. You might get a coin thrown, but with the surveillance at matches I think most of that has been done away with.'

In 1963, 17-year-old Pat Jennings made his way from Newry Town to Watford in the old Third Division. At the time he was working with his father cutting and loading timber for a firm in Newry for the princely wage of £5 a week. An Irish Junior Cup medal-winner and a Northern Ireland youth international, he was spotted by Watford scout and former Newcastle defender Bill McCracken. Offered what was then the small fortune of £15 a week, he moved to England where he made his League début for Watford against Queen's Park Rangers at the famous White City. Little did observers realise at the time that by the summer of the following year

Pat Jennings would be an established Northern Ireland senior international and also would be playing with the London giants Tottenham Hotspur.

'When I went to Watford there was a month of the season left to play,' Pat recalls. 'The team were still in danger of being relegated out of the Third Division, so they didn't take a chance by putting me in. They stuck with the goalkeeper who was already there. He played the first two matches. They couldn't be relegated after the first two matches, so I went in for the last two games. I actually played my first game for Watford against Queen's Park Rangers at the old White City. And that finished off that season.

'I played right the way through the next season. We had changed managers. Bill McGarry came in instead of a fellow called Ron Burgess, who was an ex-Tottenham player. We had a great year, missing out on promotion in the last game against Luton. That was a little bit of a disappointment, but I'd had a fantastic year. I got picked to play for the Northern Ireland team as well.

'There was a lot of paper-talk about me being linked with Tottenham and other clubs. I came home during the close-season and I got a phone call from Bill McGarry, the boss, who said: "Look, you're a young player, we want to take you back to do some extra training. I'll pick you up at the airport." He was actually there when I arrived at the airport in London. On the way back to Watford he said to me: "Do you realise what you're here for?" I said: "Well, yeah, training." "No," he said, "Mr Bill Nicholson from Tottenham is waiting to sign you at Watford." That was the first I knew about Tottenham's interest. I can remember going in that afternoon and referring to Bill Nicholson as Mr Bill Nicholson and the first thing he said to me was: "Forget about the Mister. Just call me Bill." That was unbelievable to me. Bill Nicholson was a god to me and to everybody at that time.'

By the time Pat Jennings arrived at Bill Nicholson's Spurs in the summer of 1964, the club had already won their famous Double of League Championship and FA Cup in 1960–61. Elevated to a salary of £40 a week plus £5 per first-team game, Pat stepped into the formidable boots of Scottish international Bill Brown. At the time Spurs were struggling to shed the burdensome legacy of the Double-winning team. Players came and went. Wonderful stars like Dave

Mackay, Jimmy Greaves, Cyril Knowles, Alan Mullery and Martin Chivers graced various team-sheets. Over a 13-season spell, Pat's name also was a virtual ever-present. With this sort of talent available, not surprisingly Tottenham won the FA Cup in 1967, the League Cup in 1971 and 1973, the UEFA Cup in 1972, and they also reached the UEFA Cup final in 1974 when they were defeated by Dutch side Feyenoord.

Unfortunately, the dream of a League Championship remained elusive throughout Pat Jennings' tenure with Spurs. Year after year, Bill Nicholson primed his charges for an assault on the League title. They came a creditable third on two occasions and during Pat's first ten years at the club they never slipped below halfway in the table. As a result, Pat amassed a record number of League games for Spurs without ever winning a Championship medal. In fact, by the time he left for Arsenal in August 1977, the club, which was now managed by Keith Burkinshaw, was in dire trouble and had already slid into the old Second Division.

'My career with Tottenham was unbelievable,' Pat says. 'But like everything else, because I was there as long as I was, people just take you for granted. We were going down the League instead of going up it. I think in my last year with the club I missed something like 21 or 22 games with an ankle injury and that was the year we got relegated. To be fair, the lad Barry Daines, who had come in to replace me on the team when I was out injured, had done very well. He was probably seven or eight years younger than me and he wanted to play in the first team as well. So I think it was basically a decision by the manager Keith Burkinshaw that I should go.

'My contract was up and they never offered me a new contract. I knew at that time when they weren't offering me a contract that the writing was on the wall for me. I also knew through one of our players on the Northern Ireland team that Bobby Robson of Ipswich had made an offer for me two or three months earlier. I started back in pre-season training and I played in two or three pre-season matches. Just out of the blue, one morning Keith Burkinshaw came to me and said: "Now that we've made a decision that you can go, the quicker we do it the better. I'm off to Sweden with the team tomorrow, pre-season. Bobby Robson is ringing you tonight at six o'clock and I'll ring you at half-six and I want to know where you're going." So you can guess what I said to that. I said something along the lines of: "Well, I've been here going on 14 years and you've been here two minutes, Keith. I'll let you know where I'm going in my time." It was one of those situations.

'Basically I was fixed to go down to Ipswich and they had a great team at the time. But then on the night one of his players broke his leg playing in a game in Holland, Bobby Robson rang back to say: "Sorry, the deal's off. I've got to go now and buy a forward and we can't afford to buy you." I could have gone to Manchester United. Tommy Cavanagh, who was the coach for the Northern Ireland team at the time and who was assistant to Tommy Docherty, asked me if I'd be interested in moving up to Manchester United. I could have gone to Aston Villa. There were a lot of good judges about that were still confident that I could do it. But Terry Neill, who had gone from Tottenham to Arsenal as manager, rang me during the week when it got about that I was going to be made available. And whenever I went over to Arsenal I actually signed a four-year contract. So it seems funny that one club was giving me the elbow and another club not far down the road was giving me a four-year contract.

'I remember going to the Tottenham ground to pick up my boots. I met up with three or four of the Tottenham directors and they actually ignored me on the day. I think that hurt me more than being made available. I'd spent nearly 14 years of my life at Tottenham and not one of them had the guts to say to me: "Sorry you're leaving. Thanks for being a good player for us all these years." From that minute on, I was going to suit myself. My family were able to stay in the same house. My kids didn't have to move to different schools. Plus the fact that I knew I was joining a good team at Arsenal. I knew three-quarters of the team. I knew Dave O'Leary and I played with Sammy Nelson and Pat Rice on the Irish team. So I knew I was joining a fabulous team and I knew we were definitely going to be in for winning things.'

When he joined Arsenal in 1977, Pat Jennings had already developed the reputation as one of the finest goalkeepers in Britain. By the time he had finished with the Gunners, he was regarded as arguably the greatest keeper of all time. He was fortunate that the side he joined was crammed with great stars, not least the Irish contingent of Frank Stapleton, David O'Leary, Liam Brady, Pat Rice and Sammy Nelson. Pat secured a Cup medal in the thrilling 3–2 victory over Manchester United in the 1979 FA Cup final. He played in the Arsenal sides that lost the FA Cup finals in 1978 and 1980. He also kept goal in the European Cup Winners' Cup final in 1980, when Arsenal lost to Spain's Valencia on penalties.

Throughout his time with Arsenal, Pat brought a new maturity to his game and was regarded as having the safest pair of hands ever seen in the history of football. He commanded his penalty area with a towering presence and was capable of spectacular diving saves that defied the laws of gravity. He made many saves with his feet. His one-armed catches were breathtaking. He also used his knowledge of Gaelic football, which once had him knocking on the door of the Down minor team back in the early 1960s. He was, in short, the sort of extraordinarily versatile player who was quite capable of making a brace of penalty saves, which he did against Liverpool in 1973. He also was capable of scoring at the other end with his long kick-outs, which he did against Manchester United's Alex Stepney during the Charity Shield match in 1967.

'Every save that you make in a game, if it keeps you in the game it's an important save,' Pat reflects. 'Likewise, people say to me: "What are the biggest mistakes you've made?" I've made so many of those that I can't remember many offhand. But regarding the penalty saves at Liverpool, it was so funny because when they awarded the first penalty Tommy Smith and Kevin Keegan had a race to see who was going to take it. Kevin Keegan got there first so he took it and I saved it. You can imagine the scene. Tommy was calling him all the names of the dead. We had a great laugh over this.

'Then, of course, the second one is awarded and there's nobody taking that, only Tommy Smith. Again I saved that. There are photographs of me in some books with my arms up laughing at the reaction of Smith and Keegan. Even the referee is laughing. It was funny afterwards. A lot of the press guys were interviewing Tommy Smith coming out. The match was actually played on the morning of the Grand National at Aintree and I heard him saying to the press how lucky that big Irish so-and-so was. He said that had that Irish so-and-so been riding in the Grand National that afternoon, he would have won that as well. That was Tommy Smith. They were great times and there was good banter between the lads.

'I probably scored a few own-goals in my time as well. It's one of those embarrassing situations and it's something that you dread. The thought of somebody knocking the ball from one end of the ground to the other and it hopping over the top of you is another nightmare. I think that's what happened to Alex Stepney. We were given a free kick just outside our box. Dave Mackay was more or less in his run-up to take it and I just said to Dave: "Give it to me, Dave, I'll knock it up." I hoofed it up, trying to get it to Alan Gilzean right up in the other 18-yard box. Alex came out at the back of him thinking he wouldn't control it and he would pick up a loose ball. Of course, it missed both of them and the next bounce it's in the net. The commentator on the day, Kenneth Wolstenholme, took about 30 seconds before he said: "It's a goal." Like everybody else, we were wondering what the referee would give. But it was a goal in the end, and that was it.'

The date of 25 June 1982 will forever be remembered by Northern Ireland fans, especially those who were present at the Luis Casanova Stadium in Valencia. That evening, Northern Ireland beat favourites Spain through a Gerry Armstrong goal to qualify for the second stage of the 1982 World Cup. Shocked Spanish fans, not to mention distraught World Cup organisers, struggled to come to terms with the departure of the host nation. The 150–1 outsiders from the North had defied all the odds. Pat Jennings, who played in goal that night, was an inspirational and steadying influence. In fact, ever since he won his first cap for his country while playing for Watford, he had provided a commanding presence at the heart of the Northern Ireland defence. Reaching the World Cup quarter-final stages in 1982 happened to be the pinnacle of that illustrious international career.

'I had been trying to qualify for 20 years, more or less, and you think after 20 years that it's not going to happen,' Pat says of Northern Ireland's famous World Cup campaign in 1982. 'We had a good team at the time, going out to Spain. We realised from watching earlier games that we had to be very careful with the referees and that it was important that the host nation be kept in the competition to keep the interest going within the country. When it came to Mal Donaghy getting sent off, we just couldn't believe it. Mal was probably the quietest player in our team. He never got involved with anything. He was sent off for next to nothing. But it was a fantastic night, one of the great nights. We came under a bit of pressure early on but we still felt that we'd cope with it quite easily. Then, of course, with Mal going off that put us under a little bit more pressure. But the team played well that night. Gerry Armstrong got a great goal for us and it was just one of those magic performances.'

In 1986 Pat helped Northern Ireland reach their second World Cup finals in succession, when they travelled to Mexico more in hope than expectation. Unfortunately, the North's ageing team was in decline and the glory years were all but over. Having drawn 1–1 with Algeria, the team went on to lose to Spain 2–1 and Brazil 3–0. At those 1986 World Cup finals, Pat played his last game ever in the North's defeat by Brazil. Celebrating his forty-first birthday on the day of that match, his time minding goal at both club and international levels had come to a close.

'Even way back, when I was a 32-year-old and being made surplus to requirements at Tottenham, even from that age people were writing me off,' Pat says. 'I knew myself that fitness-wise I was still as fit and as quick as anybody and that my hands were still as good as ever. I knew within myself that I could carry on.

'I always used to look at the marathon runners on television and most of them were well into their 30s and they were running 26 miles plus. I thought: "If they can run 26 miles in their 30s then I can get about the penalty box." I never had any doubt in my mind that I could keep going. In fact, even when I played my last game against Brazil in the World Cup finals in Mexico, even after that I could have played on, no problem. But I had built up a fantastic reputation over the years and you can spoil a reputation in a very short time by going down through the League. I didn't want that to happen, so that was basically the reason why I stopped playing at 41.'

At the time of his departure from international football, Pat Jennings had been playing soccer at the highest level for an extraordinary 24 years. Known as a gentle giant of football, he had developed a reputation as a calm and controlled player with a cool exterior and nerves of steel. Among Pat's treasured possessions are the Footballer of the Year and Players' Player of the Year awards won in 1973 and 1976 respectively. He also won an astonishing 119 caps for Northern Ireland. Added to his FA Cup medals won with Spurs and Arsenal, his two League Cups won with Spurs and his UEFA Cup medal also won with Spurs, he certainly had a successful career. Ultimately, however, it's for his agility, his imposing presence in goal and his command of the penalty area that Pat will long be recalled. Along with Lev Yashin of the Soviet Union and Gordon Banks of England, he is regarded as perhaps the finest goalkeeper that the game has ever produced.

'I've never seen a goalkeeper make a save that I didn't think I was capable of making,' Pat concludes. 'Whenever I look back and go through my career, I think I'm as good as anything that's gone before me. People used to say that my style of goalkeeping was unorthodox, which is an absolute load of rubbish. I could do anything as well as any other goalkeeper who had gone in front of me. It doesn't matter how. It's just a matter of keeping the ball out of the net. People used to say I made saves with my feet. So what! The feet are there. You don't have to try and get rid of your feet to get your body down. It was just the natural thing for me.

'I'd been brought up in Gaelic football. Crosses into the box, which seem to be a problem for loads of goalkeepers nowadays, were just ten-a-penny for me. They were never a problem. I think I was one of the lucky ones. I was blessed with a lot of natural talent, call it whatever you may. I'm just grateful for the career that I've had. It's nice that wherever you go throughout the world, people recognise you on the streets. They recognise you and want an autograph and it's a pleasure to be able to give them an autograph and have a chat about football.

'It's something that when you look back you can enjoy it more. When you were still involved and you had to go out and play in a couple of days' time or at the weekend, maybe you didn't enjoy winning things as much as you should have done. There was always another game coming up and you had built up a reputation and you had to live up to that the next Saturday or the next game you played. So you didn't take it in as much as you should have done. But, whenever I look back or whenever I see someone going to pick up the Footballer of the Year award or winning an FA Cup final, it's lovely to say: "Look at the mantelpiece, I've got that, I've done that, I've been there." Whenever I look back, I'm so lucky to have had the career I had.'

12. LIAM BRADY

HE ARRIVED AT JUVENTUS IN 1980, IN THE MIDDLE OF ONE OF THE CLUB'S GOLDEN eras. Under the guidance of legendary coach Giovanni Trapattoni, the Turin side was thriving. The team was a *Who's Who* of Italian soccer. Stars like Zoff, Cabrini, Gentile, Scirea, Causio, Tardelli and Bettega played in the side. The team was full of internationals. Six Juventus players formed the core of Italy's World Cup-winning side in 1982. It was that sort of set-up. The club, which had first adopted Notts County's black-and-white stripes at the turn of the century, had seldom experienced this sort of success. It was a measure of Liam Brady's standing in international soccer that he was headhunted to play in such company.

At the time, Juventus were winning scudetti like they were going out of fashion. Five scudetti had been won in the 1970s. A Coppa Italia had been secured in 1979. The UEFA Cup was won in 1977. The ambition was to achieve further success in Europe, especially in the European Cup. In the decades that followed it seemed that the Turin club would stop at nothing to realise that goal. Players like Zinedine Zidane, Roberto Baggio, Zbigniew Boniek, Michel Platini and Paolo Rossi were signed. In the early 1980s, however, it was Liam Brady who filled a similar high-profile role. In his two seasons with Juventus he delivered with style, winning two scudetti in succession, in 1981 and 1982, while becoming the club's leading goal-scorer in the 1980–81 season.

'It was a new adventure,' Liam says of his move from Arsenal to Juventus in 1980. 'I had just got married and my wife and I decided we were going to go. We really didn't know where we were going but we were going to go. I knew I was attracting enough interest from Continental clubs to find myself a good club. It was a time when

Kevin Keegan had gone to Hamburg and proved a huge success there. He'd become European Footballer of the Year whilst he was at Hamburg. It looked as if I could possibly go to Bayern Munich. That was the club that had shown most interest and that had actually talked to myself and talked to Arsenal. But for some reason, which I think had something to do with Paul Breitner saying he didn't think we could get on in the same team together, that transfer to Bayern Munich didn't come about.

'I think when I played for Arsenal against Juventus in the European Cup Winners' Cup semi-final in early 1980 I played well enough for them to say: "He's on our short list." I think they did try to go for Rummenigge at that particular time but they didn't get him. So they turned their attention to me. It all worked out very well. I went to arguably one of the most famous clubs in the world. I ended up playing with most of the team that won the 1982 World Cup. It was the start of a tremendous adventure for me and it was a tremendous experience for me in Italian football. I was going into a League that was very wealthy so the best players in the world were going to be attracted there. Before long I was playing with and against players like Sócrates, Platini, Maradona, Zico, who all went to play in Italy. It was the best move I ever made.

'I also had League success, which was something that eluded me at Arsenal. I went to a very good side at Juventus. They hadn't won the title for two or three years when I went there. I had a difficult first couple of months. It was a game against Inter Milan that really turned the whole thing around for me. I ended up scoring a goal and making another one. It was about eight games into the Championship. After that I never looked back. We went on to win the Championship. I ended up scoring eight goals for Juventus in that first season from midfield, which was good. We went on to win the title in a close race with Roma. The next year we won it again in a race with Fiorentina, beating Fiorentina by a point. So it was a great time for me.'

Liam Brady emerged from Dublin schoolboy soccer in the late 1960s. Even as a youngster he was a cut above the rest. Playing for St Kevin's Boys, he caught the attention of scouts anxious to lure new talent to England. Those were exciting days in English football. The Championship moved from club to club, with Liverpool, Manchester

United, Manchester City, Leeds United and Everton each securing the title in the five years up to 1970. By comparison, the London sides were under-performing in terms of the title race. Yet it was one of those London clubs – Arsenal – that was quick off the mark in spotting the young Liam Brady's talents. Arsenal it was, then, that Liam initially travelled to for trials as the decade came to a close.

'I first went to Arsenal in 1969 when I was 13 years of age,' Liam recalls. 'I was spotted playing in my local park for St Kevin's Boys. It was the usual scenario. A scout knocked on my door, spoke to my mother and father, said he'd been very impressed with me and would like to invite me over to play in some trial games. I did that in the summer of '69. I obviously impressed enough for them to be very interested. I was going to probably the best club at that particular time. I was very pleased with what went on there and how they treated me. That was really the start of my relationship with Arsenal.'

Fortunately for Liam, the year he finally moved full-time to Arsenal turned out to be one of the most historic in the club's history. It was 1971. Liam was aged 15. The euphoria at Highbury was palpable as the club secured a treasured Double. Arsenal edged out Leeds United in the Championship while beating Liverpool in the FA Cup. Only once before in that century had the Double been achieved – and that was by the old enemy Tottenham back in 1961. The sense of awe and admiration, the feeling of history being made, the pride in sharing such august surroundings with legendary players had a powerful impact on the young player.

'I took a great interest in the Double side,' Liam says. 'Bertie Mee was the manager. You had players like Frank McLintock, who was an inspirational captain. There was Bob Wilson, who we know from his work in the media. He was a tremendous goalkeeper. You had Pat Rice and Bob McNab as full-backs, Peter Simpson at centre-back. Up front you had John Radford, Ray Kennedy and George Armstrong. Then you had the famous Charlie George, whom I took a shine to because he was the creative player in the team. They had a really good side. It had been a good side since '69 and it went on for another four or five years.

'I knew where I was going to live because I had stayed with the people on trips over during school holidays and so forth. I settled in pretty quickly. I had family in London. My brothers Ray and Pat played for Millwall and Queen's Park Rangers. So I always had people I could go to at weekends or if I was in need of any assistance or help. If I got lonely they were always there. That was the kind of club I went to and the kind of scene it was for me as a 15-year-old boy.

'That Double side was probably 50 per cent made up of home-grown players. I think they had their youth policy up and running in a very healthy way. They were serious about getting the best players they could into the youth teams. About half a dozen of my crop of youngsters went on to play in the first team. Within a span of two or three years the likes of Frank Stapleton, David O'Leary, Graham Rix, Richie Powling, John Matthews, all went on to play for the first team. It was a good place to be a youngster at that particular time. They knew how to look after youngsters and bring them on. They had a good track record.

'When my signing worked out for them and they realised they had a good player, they thought that Dublin must be a good place to get young players. Within a year Frank Stapleton joined, then David O'Leary, John Murphy, John Devine and then Niall Quinn. We were never particularly close. We never hung around together. But we were almost like brothers in that we looked out for one another. If one of us had a problem we'd try to help and get it sorted out. It was a bit like family. Brothers don't necessarily pal around together but they look after one another. That's the way it was at Highbury at that time.'

Liam Brady made his League début for Arsenal against Birmingham City in October 1973. From the beginning, he captivated the fans. They loved his artistry and skill. They revelled in his distribution and vision. Inch-perfect passes, sweet left-footed balls, defence-splitting moves came naturally. He had brains to burn. He commanded midfield. It was clear to all those who saw him play that he was an exceptional talent. For the rest of the 1970s he built the sort of reputation that elevated him to legendary status.

For all his genius, Brady's magic wasn't enough to secure League titles for the London club. They were there or thereabouts towards the end of the '70s. Unfortunately, they were always that bit short. The FA Cup was different, with the Gunners beating Manchester United in 1979 in a final they were widely expected to lose. On either side of that victory, they lost to Ipswich Town in 1978 and to West Ham United in 1980 in finals they were expected to win. Such were the fortunes of Arsenal during Brady's years at Highbury.

There were many fine displays from Liam throughout those years. Few could match his contribution to the 1979 FA Cup final, where he initiated the move that led to Arsenal's last-gasp winner. Leading 2–0 with five minutes to go, the Gunners almost blew it when Manchester United drew level. At the death, however, Brady's inspiration indirectly led to Alan Sunderland's winner. There were disappointments too, especially Arsenal's loss to Valencia in the European Cup Winners' Cup final in 1980. Liam's missed penalty in the dramatic shootout in that match helped dash his hopes of European success. At the end, however, it didn't matter. His legacy remained untarnished. Even today, fond memories remain of a player who thrilled the fans and helped restore success to Highbury.

'We just couldn't match Leeds in the early years or Liverpool later on,' Liam says of Arsenal's failure to win the League title in his time with the club. 'Liverpool were a great team then. Shankly was the manager and then Paisley. They were just so strong. Even when they were in the process of winning a League they'd still invest in the best players that were around in the transfer market. At Arsenal we didn't do those things. I don't think the money was available then. It was a mistake because I believe, 11 against 11, Arsenal could match up with the best of them. I think we proved that in Cup games. But when it came to a long, hard season, when you needed 16, 17 or 18 players, we just didn't match the likes of Liverpool.

'The Cup games go together. In 1977–78 we began to believe in ourselves as a team. We were unlucky not to get to the final of the League Cup. Liverpool beat us in a very close two-legged semi-final. But the team began to believe in itself. And we got to the '78 Cup final. Unfortunately it coincided with injuries to the likes of Malcolm Macdonald and myself and we weren't really in good shape going into the Ipswich final. We lost 1–0 and Ipswich deservedly won the game.

'I think that stood us in good stead the next year around. We were much more focused. We were less taken up with all the razzmatazz surrounding a Cup final. We were much more concentrated on the task in hand and much more determined not to end up as losers. I think that was why we beat Manchester United on the day. In the end we were a little bit lucky in the way the game went, especially in the last few minutes. But I think the best team won on the day.

'The final one, the following year, was my last year at Arsenal. It was a major disappointment because we had a great season. We had knocked Juventus out in the semi-final of the European Cup Winners' Cup to get to the final. We lost to Valencia a few days after losing to West Ham in the FA Cup final. I think, all in all, by the time the finals came around in the space of four days – the FA Cup final and the European Cup Winners' Cup final – we just couldn't really find that spark that was needed to go and win the matches. Unfortunately we ended up losing 1–0 to West Ham and a few days later losing on penalties to Valencia.

'I had made my mind up I was leaving Arsenal. I was attracted to going abroad and seeing if I could make it abroad. It was just a sad way to end what had been a great 10 years for me. Once we had lost the European Cup Winners' Cup final it was a very sad moment. Although we had a couple of League games left to go because of our hectic season, it was the end. I had a great time at Arsenal but I wanted to move on and to test myself elsewhere.'

In the summer of 1980 Liam Brady moved from England to Italy to join Juventus. His stay in Turin lasted two seasons, after which he moved to Sampdoria, Internazionale and Ascoli. That he thrived in such company came as no surprise to those who had witnessed his performances with Arsenal. There had been some outstanding displays in his days with the Londoners. There also were wonderful games with the Republic of Ireland, beginning with his first cap back in October 1974 against the Soviet Union. In that match his partnership with Johnny Giles helped carve open the Soviet defence, resulting in a 3–0 victory. It was a dream start to a wonderful international career.

'I remember the game quite vividly,' Liam says of the Soviet Union match. 'It was a big game for me. Obviously I wasn't in the squad that long because I was so young. Then Johnny Giles threw me in at the deep end against the Soviet Union. It was really the beginning of the Giles' era. He'd had a couple of games before that. I think he'd had an end-of-season tour to South America. He had his ideas set on the team, how they were going to play. He threw me in at the deep end and we got off to a great start by beating the Soviet Union 3–0 at Dalymount Park.

'When we kicked off, the ball went to John and John gave the ball to me almost as if to say: "There you go. I've got the utmost confidence in you. Let's go and play." And we did. Don Givens got a tremendous hat-trick on the day. It was probably one of the games that I'll always remember. There's maybe a handful in your career that you can remember vividly. That would be one of them.'

The emergence of Liam Brady was a godsend for the international side, which moved to a new level under the managerial guidance of Johnny Giles and later Eoin Hand. The team was exciting to watch, with the Arsenal trio of Brady, Stapleton and O'Leary lining out, at various times, alongside quality players like Steve Heighway, Don Givens, Mark Lawrenson, Gerry Daly and, of course, Johnny Giles. There were wonderful matches, including a 1–0 victory over France in 1977, with the winning goal scored by Liam Brady. Over the years, however, some disappointing refereeing decisions denied Brady the chance to perform on a bigger stage. The talent was wonderful. The organisation was admirable. Unfortunately, the breakthrough failed to occur.

'It was so near and yet so far,' Liam says. 'We couldn't quite make that breakthrough. We had some great performances, great results along the way. But we were never really fortunate enough to get the breaks when we needed them. It didn't work out until Jack Charlton came along. With him, we began to get the breaks that we hadn't had. For example, qualifying for the European Championship in 1988, we all thought even after beating Bulgaria 2–0 in Dublin that we were out. But Scotland went and got a miraculous result in Sofia and there we were, centre-stage, among only eight teams in the European Championship. That tells you how hard it was to qualify. And that was the start of Ireland getting on the international football map.'

The arrival of manager Jack Charlton in 1986 didn't quite end Liam Brady's international career in the manner that many recall. Although his role changed under Charlton's more direct tactical style, he still made a crucial contribution to the international side's successful campaigns. He was central to the Republic of Ireland's progress in the Euro '88 qualifiers. Unfortunately, the combination of a red card against Bulgaria in October 1987 and a career-threatening injury denied him a place in the European Championship finals in West Germany.

Any chance of making up for that misfortune by claiming a place in the panel for Italia '90 came abruptly to an end in September 1989. It happened after Liam was somewhat insensitively substituted during the Republic of Ireland's friendly against West Germany. Following West Germany's equaliser, Brady was immediately withdrawn. It was the final nail in the coffin for a player who was, at the time, in the twilight of his career with West Ham United. His last appearance for the Republic of Ireland was in his testimonial against Finland in May 1990, following which he departed the scene with a total of 72 caps. Sadly, there would be no World Cup finals for Liam Brady.

'It was disappointing for me,' Liam agrees. 'You sense when your time is up or when a manager favours you, or when a manager is supportive of you. I played really well for Jack. I played in all the games in the Euro '88 campaign. I started off the campaign playing for Ascoli in Italy. That didn't last too long. I fell out with them and I ended up coming back to West Ham. We played against Scotland, Bulgaria and Belgium. I got off to a good start under Jack in Belgium, where we drew 2–2. I scored an equaliser in the last few minutes from the penalty spot. We beat Brazil in Dublin at the time. I was lucky enough to get the goal. I was playing really well for Jack.

'In the last game I got sent off against Bulgaria. It was my own fault. I retaliated. A guy had been giving me some rough treatment and I retaliated. I didn't think it was going to be too costly because I didn't think we were going to qualify. Little did I know then that we'd get a break. I got my sentence reduced from four games to two games, which gave me a chance of playing in the competition. Just after that I ruptured my cruciate ligament playing for West Ham. So that was the end of that.

'After that, Andy Townsend began to come into the team just after the European Championship. Jack felt he was more suited to the way he wanted the game played. I was on the periphery of things and I knew my time had come. That was it. It was a sad way to go. Maybe with another manager, with another style of play, he would have wanted Liam Brady in the squad to go to Italy. But it wasn't to be. I knew my time was up. Having been substituted at Lansdowne Road against West Germany, I said: "I've had enough. Good luck. Do well. And thanks for the memories."

'My regret is not so much the 1990 World Cup because I was 34 then and I was past my best. My regret was that we weren't lucky enough, or didn't get enough breaks, to have played in a World Cup under Johnny Giles, with the team that he had then. He had a good side with Don Givens up front, Gerry Daly, Dave O'Leary and Frank Stapleton breaking through, all in their prime. I think '78 or '82 are my regrets that we didn't make it then. I regret the European Championship in '88 because when you play in all the qualifying rounds and you play really well, and you finally get there after 14 years of playing for your country and it doesn't happen for you, that's a big regret as well. But by the time 1990 had come around I had become a supporter and I was just happy that we'd finally made that big breakthrough.'

Phrases like 'world-class' are usually used to describe Liam Brady's football skills. Without any doubt, he was one of a tiny number of Irish players who could justify such acclaim. At Arsenal alone, he is still spoken of with reverence and awe, which is hardly surprising given that he was, on three occasions, selected by the fans as Player of the Year. He also was selected as PFA Player of the Year in 1979. Not surprisingly, Arsenal fans remember him with the utmost of affection.

Likewise, Liam's Italian adventure is remembered not only for the success he achieved but also for the quality of football he produced while playing at the highest level. The Italians loved him. He is a legend in Turin. Although he subsequently went into management with Celtic and Brighton, it is for his contribution to the many clubs he served as a player that Liam is so fondly recalled. Whether at Arsenal, Juventus, Internazionale, Sampdoria, Ascoli or West Ham United, there was no better exponent of the art of midfield play.

'Regarding how good a player you are and how successful you are, both are measured by the amount of time you stuck around at the very highest level,' Liam concludes. 'I started off at a very high level with Arsenal and I was successful there. Then I went to Italy and had great success initially. Then I dropped down a rung when I went to Sampdoria but bounced back again when I went to Inter Milan. To play the best part of 15 years at the highest level is a test. It proves that you were successful in your career. To have six of those years at the very highest level in Italy, with the players I've mentioned, playing with the World Cup winners and playing with some of the best players in the world, was an experience that was well worth it.'

13. NORMAN WHITESIDE

HE WAS, BY ANY STANDARDS, A FOOTBALL PHENOMENON. AT 16 HE MADE HIS FIRST-team début as a sub for Manchester United. Just turned 17 he scored in his first full match. Also at 17 he smashed Pelé's record to become the youngest player to appear in a World Cup finals. Still aged 17, he scored in the League Cup final against Liverpool. At just 18 he was the youngest player to score in a FA Cup final, against Brighton. There seemed to be no stopping this extraordinary teenager in the early 1980s.

Born in Belfast and brought up on the Shankill Road, by the age of seven Norman Whiteside was already banging in goals for his Boys' Brigade team. Sometimes he hammered in 10 or more goals in a match. For his school he scored around 100 goals in one season alone. Picked for the Northern Ireland schoolboys, he was soon promoted to captain. Clubs in England started to chase him. Ipswich Town came knocking. So too did Manchester United. United won and the records started to tumble. Strong and well built, he became, like George Best before him, a legend at Old Trafford.

'I first went across when I was a youngster,' Norman recalls. 'They liked what they saw. Eventually I was going to Belfast Airport every Friday night, flying over and playing for the juniors on a Saturday and flying back on a Sunday. I had the skinhead haircut, the Doc Martins and I had the duffle-coat. You'd want to see the looks I was getting from the commuters with the bowler hats. Here was this little skinhead with a pair of boots over his shoulder. They didn't know I was going over to play for Manchester United juniors. That brought me through to when I became an apprentice professional.'

Working his way through the 'A' and 'B' teams, Norman Whiteside showed he could mix it with the best at Old Trafford. He was soon sharing dressing-rooms with hardened professionals in the reserve side, showing no fear and much skill as he settled in with the rest of the team. Those were grim enough days in the club's history. With Ron Atkinson as manager, the team struggled to regain the sort of League prominence that was last seen in the 1960s. By 1981–82 it was clear to Atkinson that new blood was required. That fresh injection of youthful energy and talent was made in April 1982 when the 16-year-old Norman Whiteside was introduced as a sub against Brighton. For the young teenager from Belfast it marked the start of a magnificent era.

'The boss called me in,' Norman recollects. 'He said: "Go and get your suit, you're travelling with the first team." I think he knew I had only one suit at the time. So off we went and there was a bit of speculation when we woke up in the morning that this 16-year-old boy might be making his début. But when Big Ron named his team I was substitute.

'I got on for the last 12 minutes. Ray Wilkins scored a great goal and we won the game 1–0. The funny thing about it, which people find hard to believe, is that I was on £16 a week at the time. The win bonus that day was £800. I was substitute for a few games and then I made my full début after that. We won them all. So I collected over £3,000 in win bonuses and I was only on £16 a week. I thought I had won the lottery.

'My full début was against Stoke City at Old Trafford. I think Bryan Robson scored and I scored. We won that one, as I said. After that we went to America. The manager said: "Norman, be at the airport in the morning at nine o'clock with your passport. You're going on the first-team tour to Canada." I couldn't believe it. I thought: "Boss, this is fantastic." He said: "I'm only taking you under one condition." I said: "What's that, boss?" He said: "That you drink Canada Dry." So I gave it my best shot, if you know what I mean.'

Norman Whiteside returned from Canada just in time to join Northern Ireland for their historic 1982 World Cup campaign. Having missed the hard slog of the qualifying rounds, he was selected for the finals in Spain. Chosen by manager Billy Bingham for the opening match against Yugoslavia, Norman became the youngest player ever to play in a World Cup finals. Aged 17 years and 41 days, he surpassed the record set by Pelé back in 1958. He also played a major role in Northern Ireland's progress in the competition, helping them defeat Spain on home territory while advancing to the quarter-finals. Comparisons with the young George Best's explosive arrival in football in the early 1960s were inevitable.

'That was a great thrill to beat the world-famous Pelé's record,' Norman says. 'But it didn't really hit home to me at that particular time how big the occasion was because obviously I'd just come on the scene. I'd only been in Manchester United's first team for a couple of appearances and then I'm in the World Cup alongside Sammy McIlroy, Pat Jennings, Jimmy Nicholl, people like that. They're saying: "Norman, do you realise, son, that we've been through all our careers just looking for this and you're starting your career in a World Cup?"

'The one thing that I do remember from the World Cup is the media attention, which probably would be similar to what's going around these days. In those days I had every single country that was involved in world football wanting to interview me because I'd beaten Pelé's record. That was quite tricky for a young kid going into a game because first and foremost I couldn't speak all the languages. They were asking me questions in different languages and it was quite weird really. All I wanted to do was play football. Luckily enough I played in all our five games in that World Cup and we went on to beat the host nation Spain to go through to the quarter-final stage.

'Comparisons with George Best were inevitable. It was always going to happen. I was actually quoted once and I said: "Look, apart from both George and I coming from Belfast, apart from both of us going to Manchester United, apart from both of us being spotted by the same scout Bob Bishop, apart from both of us liking a few beers, we've absolutely nothing in common." But the media attention was really big in terms of comparing me to Best because of coming from the same place and so on. I really was single-minded and determined not to let it bother me and they soon got away from it. You only have to look and you can see that no one can lace George's boots, the genius he was. I'd love to have been a quarter of the player George Best was. The other daft thing about it was that we had two completely different playing styles anyway. So it was just newspaper talk, which didn't upset me. But you just wish these things wouldn't have happened.'

Within 12 months Norman Whiteside was back in the spotlight when he played with Manchester United in the 1983 FA Cup final

IRELAND'S SOCCER TOP 20

against Brighton. Brighton were relegated that season. Manchester United came third in the League. The disparity between the teams didn't stop Brighton from almost snatching victory at Wembley Stadium. After unluckily being held to a 2–2 draw in the showcase match in May, Brighton eventually succumbed to a 4–0 drubbing by the Reds in the replay. Having scored one of the goals, Norman Whiteside became the youngest player ever to score in a FA Cup final. Only a few months before that, he had become the youngest player ever to score in a Wembley Cup final when scoring in United's ill-fated League Cup decider against Liverpool.

'I scored in the semi-final of the FA Cup against Arsenal at Villa Park and that took us through to the final that year,' Norman recollects. 'We drew the first one 2–2 and were very lucky indeed. I think it was Gordon Smith who missed a sitter just before the end and we were fortunate to get the replay. In the replay we showed our true class and went on to beat them 4–0. Bryan Robson scored two, I scored one and Arnold Muhren scored a penalty. I've got all these silly little titles, well they're not silly, but all these lovely little titles of the youngest this and the youngest that. That one made me the youngest ever to score in a FA Cup final, at the age of 18 years and 19 days, something like that.'

Over the next two years Norman Whiteside enhanced his reputation by helping Manchester United to successive top-four finishes in the League. Although it was clearly not enough for those who pined for the glory days, the pain was eased somewhat by another FA Cup triumph in 1985. With Everton as opponents the omens weren't promising. After all, Everton were Charity Shield winners and had just wrapped up the Championship. However, although Kevin Moran was sent off in the final, Manchester United battled hard to secure another FA Cup victory, by the score of 1–0. And who should score the winning goal other than Norman Whiteside!

'We came up against Everton, who were then going for the Treble,' Norman recalls. 'We knew it was going to be a tough game but from what I remember of it, all those years ago, it wasn't a great game. I don't think the football was very good. But, at the end of the day, we just stuck at it and then Kevin Moran got sent off. Everybody just sort of looked at each other and you could see it in our eyes that we really wanted to do something extra. We pulled it together.

'Fortunately in the extra-time period Mark Hughes fed me with a great ball. I was stuck out in the right wing because I was getting back from the previous attack. I was so tired. I said: "Leave me out of this one." I just stayed on the right wing and Mark Hughes fed me the ball. I actually used to practise using a defender as a screen, with the goalkeeper, the defender and myself in a perpendicular straight line. When I looked up the defender wasn't in that perpendicular straight line. Then I threw my leg over the ball and at that particular time he came into that line so Neville Southall was obstructed. As tired as I was, at the back of my mind something said: "Hit it, Norman." So there was a bit of theory behind it really. People have said to me: "Norman, did you mean that as a cross?" But it was definitely meant as a shot.'

Even back in the early 1980s, in the days before the proliferation of agents, each new season brought speculation concerning the movement of players into and out of Old Trafford. As far back as 1983 Norman Whiteside was being tipped as a transfer target. Much of the speculation concerned AC Milan, which was a team still some years away from its great European Cup successes of 1989 and 1990. Speculation soon turned into a concrete proposal. After displaying his talents with Northern Ireland in world football, Norman Whiteside was presented with the offer of a move to Milan.

'I could have gone,' Norman says. 'There were lots of offers in from Europe. The biggest one was from AC Milan, who had offered Manchester United £1.5 million for my services. I think I was 18 and AC Milan had offered me like £1 million as a signing-on fee and so on. Big Ron said to me: "Norman, you can speak to them and you can go if you want. We'll have you back if it doesn't work out." It was that type of arrangement. I thought: "Well, I haven't even proved myself really at Old Trafford." I loved the club. When you're starting your career you always think you're going to stay there all your life, especially at the biggest club in the world like United. I wasn't ready. I was, like I say, only 18. I didn't give it much consideration, regardless of the money. I just got on with it. I said: "Boss, I'd rather play for Manchester United." I think he put me in the reserves after that!'

Despite his obvious talent and goal-scoring prowess, there was no doubting the sheer physicality of Norman Whiteside's football style. The intense concentration and commitment he showed in games were matched by his rock-solid physical appearance. Even from his early years he not only towered over his peers but he also dominated them with his bodily strength and aggression. It was an attribute that didn't always win him admirers, especially among opposing players and fans. Referees also were known to disapprove of his forceful style, earning him a not inconsiderable number of bookings.

'I was a very stubborn type of player,' Norman reflects. 'I'm probably a stubborn person as well. All I had as a goal in my life was to be a footballer. At three o'clock I didn't go around beating walls and kicking doors and listening to ghetto-blasters. I just sat there. I had done my homework the night before in my bedroom, just lying there, concentrating mentally on what way the game was going to go. Then I went out and did my job from three o'clock until the end whistle.

'People might have said I was dirty but I just think I was competitive. The biggest thing that brought me a lot of yellow cards, which I do admit to, was my lack of pace. When I used to lift my reports up after getting booked, the only words that stuck out in every report were: "Intended to injure a player." That was because the player always got there before me and it looked clumsier than I actually meant it to be. I know in my own heart that I never went into any tackle to hurt anyone and I didn't have any black books or anything like that. But I liked to think I played the game hard and competitively because, after all, that's what it's about.'

In 1986 Norman Whiteside was part of the Northern Ireland squad that made it to the World Cup finals in Mexico. There the team performed with dignity although they failed to make it past the first round. Back in Manchester the seasons seemed to roll from one into the other as United struggled in vain to win the coveted League Championship title. Players came and went. Managers eventually changed too, with Alex Ferguson replacing Ron Atkinson in November 1986. His arrival at the club was followed by tabloid tales of excess among players like Paul McGrath and Norman Whiteside. Norman was experiencing injury and fitness problems as well. But those rumours of drinking and socialising dominated proceedings as Ferguson got to grips with the club.

'Me and Paul used to live in digs together,' Norman explains. 'That was unbelievable, that was. It was good *craic*. We used to have a good time. I've never hidden the fact that I like a good time. I like socialising. But I am being very honest when I say that I always did it at the right time. I never did it on a Thursday and Friday before a game or on a Monday and Tuesday before a Wednesday game. What I would say is that like anybody else, any guy that goes to work Monday to Friday, they go out and have a good weekend. We were entitled to do the same.

'We used to go out and have a good Saturday night and a good Sunday lunch and really enjoy that time. One particular year all the newspapers were giving Paul, Bryan Robson and myself a lot of stick about drinking and wild nights. We were actually followed at one stage by I'm not sure which tabloid. It was one of those papers you'd eat fish and chips out of. They used to follow us around. One of them followed me for I don't know how long. But they didn't get any real scandal.

'That season it was the Rest of the World against the Football League for the centenary at Wembley and who was picked but Robson, Whiteside and McGrath! You look at that game at Wembley. We played against all the best players in the world like Maradona. You name them. Robbo scored two, I scored one and Paul got Man of the Match. So we were drinking something right, weren't we? I think we were professional enough to do the job. Big Ron said in the past that we were some of the first on his team-sheets. You can only go by that.'

At the start of the 1989–90 season Norman Whiteside was transferred from Manchester United to Everton. There had been rumours of moves to other English or Continental sides but the deal was finally sealed with the Merseyside club for an initial fee of £600,000 plus an extra £150,000 following an agreed number of games. Interestingly, the transfer was closely accompanied by the sale of Paul McGrath to Aston Villa. In one fell swoop Alex Ferguson had offloaded the two players who had become, it was rumoured, very much surplus to the manager's requirements at Old Trafford.

'There's been a lot of speculation about my move from Manchester United to Everton,' Norman says. 'I'm quite clear and blunt about that as well. I was on my last legs with injuries and Alex and me had a good chat. I'm not hiding the fact that he disciplined us a few times as well and everybody thinks he got rid of me and Paul because of the drink and so on. I can't speak for Paul. I can only speak for myself. And I know that I sat in the office with Alex and we both believed it would be good if I moved.

'The other side of the story is that when you're a youngster at a football club you're not as well paid as the incoming superstars are. To put all of that in perspective I can tell you that I actually went to Everton and earned more money at Goodison Park in two years than I did in my entire Manchester United career. So it was good financially for me. I probably would have been a bit bitter from the game, having gone through all my operations and putting tireless amounts of work in, if I had come out of the game without something. So that was a little bit of security at the end of the day.'

In his first season at Goodison Park, Norman Whiteside continued to score goals and was well pleased with his performances for Everton. It all looked so promising as the 1990–91 season began. Everton were solidly established in the First Division. The pressures that Norman had experienced at United had all but disappeared. But then came what was literally a crushing blow to his career. It happened as a result of a tackle at a training-session held on 20 September 1990. It proved to be the end of the road for Norman Whiteside. Aged 25, his career was all but over.

'I ended up my career having something like 11 operations in total,' Norman says. 'When you have operations and when you come back, you always end up having little secondary injuries, muscular injuries and so on. I started to pick up quite a few injuries early on in my career and, knowing what I know now having finished, a lot of it can be down to playing too much football too soon, even younger than when I started with United. In my first season I played 55 or 56 games at 17. That's at the highest level. Well before that, at schoolboy level, at 13 or 14, there are lots of kids playing too much football. If they ever make it or if they ever go on in their careers, it can catch up with them.

'The final injury was just a clumsy little tackle in training. My knee went one way and I went the other way. I thought: "I've gone through this once too many times." My knee had a lot of operations and I knew this seemed a bit worse. I rehabilitated and it just wouldn't come back. At the end of the day the biggest thing that made my decision for me was that I wasn't playing to the standards that I'd set myself. Norman Whiteside had standards when he played football and I couldn't reach those standards.

'I could have easily sat at Goodison for an extra two years on a great contract and taken the money and played in the reserves and just played easy. Reserve football and first-team football are a million miles apart. I could have done that. But I was honest with the club and we sat around the table and we negotiated a pay-off. That's where the end came and I was only 26. So I decided to go back to school and educate myself after that.

'I had all those operations and injuries and I became familiar with some of the muscles and parts of the body and it fascinated me. I got to like the medicine side of football. I was interested and if you find things interesting then it's easier to learn. I didn't have any formal qualifications whatsoever so I went back to school and did some GCSEs, some A-levels and then did a full-time podiatry course.'

After all his youthful endeavours and achievements, it was somewhat ironic that Norman Whiteside's career ended in his mid-20s. He departed with two FA Cup medals and a total of 38 caps for Northern Ireland. He also left behind memories of a *Roy of the Rovers* rise to fame, reflecting the dreams and aspirations of young boys who believe that they too might some day play at Old Trafford at the age of 16. That Norman did so was in itself a major achievement. That he became a teenage legend while playing in World Cup finals and FA Cup finals was a remarkable triumph. Perhaps it explains why even today, long after his star has faded, he is so fondly regarded by fans at Old Trafford.

'I look back on it thinking it's better to be a has-been than not to have been at all,' Norman concludes. 'We were at Aston Villa once and I went for a wee and the next thing I was on a team of shoulders. I had managed to put my willy away at the time so I didn't wee over them. But they were all chanting and chanting and putting me on their shoulders. It's good to get a little bit of adulation now and again. But I certainly don't miss the pressure the boys are under these days.

'I could find much to look at and say I'm bitter because I could have gone on to make millions and be on £20,000 a week and win the Championship and do this, that and the other. But I look on the positive side of things and think that I've had 10 good years and I've made a few headlines. I've had some happy times and I'd rather look at those than look at what might have happened. Certainly I wouldn't regret anything or change anything that's happened in my life so far. I've had an enjoyable one.'

14. RONNIE WHELAN

THE REACTION OF THE FANS SAID IT ALL. STUNNED DISBELIEF WAS WRITTEN ON THEIR faces. They were shell-shocked. They had never before seen a goal quite like it scored by an Irish player. There were 15,000 Irish supporters in the crowd of 45,000. They were incredulous, mouths open, minds racing, trying to take it all in. And there before them was Ronnie Whelan, down on his knees, arms raised in triumph, joy written all over his features, about to be swamped by his team-mates having scored a goal of Brazilian quality.

That day in Hanover, Ronnie Whelan manufactured one of the finest strikes in the history of Irish soccer. The occasion was the 1988 European Championship finals. The Republic of Ireland's opponents were the Soviet Union. In the first match they had beaten England 1–0 courtesy of a goal from Ray Houghton. Now they were 1–0 ahead against the Soviet Union thanks to a piece of magic from the Liverpool wizard. From a long throw-in by McCarthy, Ronnie had spectacularly volleyed the ball into Dasaev's net. It was inch-perfect, instinctive and redolent of skills more familiar to the South Americans than to Jack Charlton's Republic of Ireland.

'We'd been practising it in training for about a week,' Ronnie says with a laugh. 'That's a lie. It was just something that happened. We were playing well against the Soviet Union and everybody was up for the game. We were passing the ball. We weren't kicking it, as we usually did. People were relaxed. We had beaten England. It was a throw-in. Mick McCarthy went and took it in their right full-back position. I would usually, if Mick had a throw-in there, be supporting it or standing in midfield. But for some reason I found myself on the edge of the box and the big midfielder Mikhailichenko, who went to Rangers afterwards, was picking me up.

'I feinted to make a run and come back inside. The ball just appeared. Mick had thrown it about 40 yards and it came out of the sky nicely. I thought: "Why not? People can only laugh at you if you fall over and miss it." I didn't even catch it right. It more or less caught me on the top of my foot and the bottom of my shin, that sort of area. It didn't fly in at all but sort of looped into the top corner. I remember running to the crowd that day and there was a look of surprise on people's faces that it had gone in. That was one thing that has stuck with me all the time. People were looking at each other in the crowd going: "Did that go in?" But that was probably the best thing that ever happened to me playing with Ireland.'

It came as no surprise that Ronnie Whelan played such a spectacular role during the 1988 European Championship finals. At the time of his strike against the Soviet Union, he was at the peak of his powers. In fact, throughout the 1980s and into the start of the '90s, he shared in a remarkable six League titles with Liverpool. He also was part of Liverpool's European Cup success in 1984. Two FA Cups and three League Cups completed the picture. Few Irish players could even come close to matching Ronnie Whelan's haul of silverware with Liverpool.

Born in Dublin in 1961, Ronnie seemed genetically groomed for football success. His father, also called Ronnie Whelan, had played for the Republic of Ireland in the 1960s. Although the younger Ronnie made a name for himself with Home Farm, he wisely took his time before moving cross-channel. Having completed his Leaving Certificate, he was eventually signed by Bob Paisley at the age of 18. Even in hindsight, it was a risky move. Here was a young hopeful joining a club whose trophy-cabinet was stuffed with League Championships and European Cups won in the 1970s. The club, however, was homely, close to Dublin and clearly geared for continued success.

'It was a great place to be at that time,' Ronnie recalls of his first months at Anfield in 1979. 'I suppose every club when it's successful is a good place to be. There was a good family atmosphere. That was one of the reasons I wanted to go there. You could join in with the first team and have a laugh. You had mixed games every Monday morning with the first team, kids and reserves. So you were always in touching distance. The first team was not millions of miles away from you.

'I did say to my dad before I went: "I don't know if I can make it at Liverpool." They had players like Terry McDermott, Sammy Lee, Graeme Souness and Kenny Dalglish there at the time. He said: "Well, you may as well go and start at the top. If you don't make it then you can look to a smaller club or a little less than Liverpool." So I basically took a chance. But it was a bit daunting when you saw the likes of the players that were there. They were winning League Championships and European Cups all the time.

'On my first day I met Bob Paisley and people like that. You're in Anfield, you see the trophy-room that's there, the big trophy-room upstairs. There are pictures in corridors of top players picking up European Cups and League Championships. You are in awe of the place. I thought: "I'm 18, can I do it here?" But my dad said: "If you play with better players you become a better player yourself." And that proved to be true.'

In April 1981 Ronnie Whelan made his first-team début for Liverpool in a victory over Stoke City. It proved to be a great occasion for the Dubliner, who scored in his very first game. His mum and dad were there to witness the event. Replacing Ray Kennedy in the team he was thrilled with the outcome. That season, however, the club could only manage fifth in the League, which was their worst placing in a decade. They also got knocked out of the FA Cup. Yet they did beat Real Madrid in the European Cup final in May, which was a not-inconsiderable achievement. However, what mattered to the young Ronnie Whelan was that he had somehow squeezed himself into the picture, at last getting a game alongside the galaxy of stars gracing Anfield.

'I made my début on a Friday night,' Ronnie remembers. 'It was Grand National weekend. They used to play Friday night or Saturday morning before the Grand National. This one was a Friday night. I was at the Thursday meeting at Aintree with Kevin Sheedy, who I was in digs with at the time. When we got back to the digs after the races the landlady said: "You've got to report for training tomorrow with your gear, to go to the game." I thought she was talking to Kevin because he was the one who was tipped to play in the first team. Fortunately she was talking to me.

'I went training with the first team the next morning. I went to the hotel in the afternoon thinking I was just there as the odd man out.

They always put an extra one in the squad. But Ray Kennedy was injured. So I was given the nod on the left side of midfield. Again it was like: "God, what am I doing here?"

'Fortunately it went all right. My dad said I'd play better with better players and I did. After 20 minutes I latched onto a ball. I ran what seemed about a mile and a half at the time, but I think it was about 40 yards. I just touched it underneath the keeper to score on my début. So it was a big night. My mum and dad were over for the game and the Grand National the next day. But we ended up getting the first flight back to Dublin the next morning and partied for the weekend back in Dublin.'

At the turn of the 1980s it seemed impossible for Liverpool to maintain the extraordinary pace set in the previous decade. Four League titles had been secured in the '70s. Back-to-back European Cup victories had been achieved in 1977 and 1978. Two UEFA Cups and one FA Cup were also secured. This was no ordinary run of success. Wonderful players like John Toshack, Kevin Keegan, Kenny Dalglish, Emlyn Hughes, Steve Heighway, Alan Hansen and Ray Clemence played for the club. When a star player began to wilt and fade, in came new blood. When Keegan left, in came Dalglish. Make no mistake but in the 1970s Liverpool were one of the great forces in world football.

If Liverpool's opponents hoped for a downturn in the club's fortunes in the 1980s, they were in for a big surprise. Liverpool won the League Championship in 1982 with Ronnie Whelan a virtual ever-present in the side. Overall, the club won six League Championships in the '80s. They also won the European Cup in 1984, beating Roma on penalties. They won four League Cups in a row from 1981 to 1984. They added two FA Cups in 1986 and 1989. The continuity was awesome. First Joe Fagan and later Kenny Dalglish seamlessly replaced Bob Paisley in the manager's chair. Being part of this relentless football machine was a dream come true for the club's Irish star.

'We had players like Phil Neal, Phil Thompson, Alan Hansen and we had Souness, Dalglish, Terry McDermott at the start,' Ronnie recollects. 'They were great players and you couldn't but learn from them. It wasn't just on the pitch but what they did off the pitch, how they looked after themselves and behaved themselves. You'd watch players like Souness, Dalglish and Hansen to see what they did when we were away on pre-season, when they'd go to bed, how they'd behave after a game. You'd learn from all that. Dalglish was in bed probably every afternoon. I took a lot from that. I slept an awful lot in the afternoons just to get myself ready for a Saturday. You can have a pint on a Saturday if you want but during the week you had got to look after yourself. I found going to bed very beneficial for me. That is what I learned from them, mainly what to do off the pitch. You've got the ability to play football so if you look after yourself you'll be OK on the day.

'The main thing is that we always had good players. In the time I was there they'd always bring in two a season, three at the most. They never made wholesale changes and bring six or seven in. Maybe one season they'd buy Mark Lawrenson or Michael Robinson, or something like that. But that would be it. Paul Walsh would come in. It was never big changes. The players they brought in always fitted into the system that we played, which was mainly passing the ball. They didn't like to kick long balls but if the need arose they did it. When you go back to the '80s there were lots of days when the pitches were bad. So there were days when we had to kick long balls and just follow them and scrap for a point or scrap to win games. But overall the main thing was that we had good players.

'There also was the boot-room mentality. They had a tried and trusted way regarding how they won things. It got a bit monotonous at times. We probably did the same training every day of every week. But we played a lot of football games and that broke up the monotony, playing seven-a-sides, which we found great. But with Bob, Joe, Kenny, who were the main managers, if things were going wrong they'd go back in the book. They kept a book of what they did every day and how the game went on a Saturday. They'd go back in the book and say: "Hang on, we did this two years ago, let's go back to this." And they'd get the run going again.

'Everyone knew – Bob, Joe, Kenny – what the others before had done and they didn't do much different. They just kept pushing it along nicely. Kenny was probably the one who signed more players in a season. He saw he needed something and he brought in four players, which was a lot for one season for Liverpool. He brought in

Barnes, Beardsley, Aldridge and Ray Houghton. It was great. There was a continuity to the whole thing.'

Although he played in midfield, Ronnie Whelan demonstrated a remarkable ability to score goals for Liverpool. He often did so in games of crucial importance when the chips were down and the pressure was on. In the 1982 League Cup final against Spurs his late equaliser brought the game into extra-time. A second goal from Ronnie and another from Ian Rush secured a 3–1 victory. The following season against Manchester United he again scored the crucial goal in Liverpool's 2–1 League Cup triumph. With the instincts of a natural predator, his scoring record was an added string to his bow throughout Liverpool's extraordinary decade in the 1980s.

'I was fairly fortunate that I scored in a lot of semi-finals and Cup finals,' Ronnie remarks. 'They were goals that people remember. I wasn't a prolific goal-scorer. But I did score important goals. It started off early on in my first League Cup final when I got two against Tottenham. Then the next League Cup final I got one against Manchester United, which won the game. People start to look at you. I read an article recently that Bob Paisley wrote about big games. Bob said that while reporters would be saying Kenny or someone might score he would always look past them because Ronnie could always pop up and score a goal. I think it was just more luck than being in Cup finals. I would say I was fortunate although other people would say: "He did it on the big stage." But you had to be in the right place at the right time.'

In sharp contrast to his career at Liverpool, Ronnie Whelan emerged on the international stage just in time to savour the Republic of Ireland's disappointments in the early 1980s. He made his first appearance, against Czechoslovakia, in a friendly at Lansdowne Road in 1981. He played in the massive 3–2 win over France in the World Cup qualifiers later that year. He continued to make appearances under the stewardship of Eoin Hand up to the manager's demise in late 1985. Once Jack Charlton took over in 1986, however, Ronnie's standing in the international pecking-order rose appreciably. From then on, especially in the 1988 European Championship finals, his name was inextricably linked with the Republic of Ireland's football revival.

Unfortunately for Ronnie, his ventures at Italia '90 were curtailed through a mixture of injury and the whims of the manager. Likewise, Ronnie's role at USA '94 was tragically interrupted by the long list of injuries that overshadowed his final years as a footballer. However, nobody can forget his contribution to the Republic of Ireland's performances at the European Championship finals in 1988. He played in all three matches in West Germany. Although the team took an early flight home, Ronnie left behind memories of that wonderful goal he scored in the 1–1 draw with the Soviet Union. There were other great performances during his 53 appearances for his country but none can match that magical moment in Hanover in June 1988.

'When I came into the squad under Eoin I started off all right,' Ronnie says of his early international career. 'I came on against Czechoslovakia and we beat them 3–1 in Dublin. That was my début. Then I played against France, played in midfield, played all right and was full of running. But then I was getting injuries and not getting in the team. I felt a bit alienated in the squad, which was an older squad. Liam Brady was there. Also Mick Martin and Gerry Daly were there. They were all a bit older than me. So I did feel a bit alienated in that squad at times, especially when I wasn't in it. I pulled out of a lot of squads, a lot of times injured, a lot of times concentrating on getting myself fit again to play for Liverpool.

'Once Jack took over I was playing regularly in midfield. We were winning all the time. That's when I really enjoyed it. I was happier. I wanted to turn up. It was a good atmosphere. We had a squad of about 25 or 26 players and you were happy to be in their company. We had a good laugh. I enjoyed winning although the football side of it was a bit alien to me. Kicking long balls over the full-backs' heads was not what we did at Liverpool. We did the complete opposite. But if you wanted to be part of it, you had to join in.

'I didn't like it most of the time. But if you didn't do it, you weren't in the team. That was Jack's philosophy. But it got success so you can't really knock it. Sometimes I wonder would we have got more success and could we have been even better because we had some very good football players at that time. We'll never know. But I do think about it a lot, that we may have done things differently and been better. Who's to know?

'From when Jack took over until the World Cup in 1990

everything was rosy. But then I got injuries and I wasn't in the team. It started before the World Cup. I played nearly every game in the qualifying rounds. But I got an injury just before the World Cup finals. I went away with the squad and I was trying to get fit. We were in Malta acclimatising and I was getting fit. We were doing training, where the ball is pushed ahead of you and you go through and have a shot. I felt something go in my thigh when I hit it. I struggled with that, trying to get in shape all the time.

'Eventually I got myself fairly fit. We played a game out in Italy, I think just before the Egypt game. Jack tried to play three centre-backs for the first team. I played on the opposite team and I think we were about 3–0 up after 20 minutes or so. I was feeling sharp. I was playing well. So I expected myself to be in at least the subs for the Egypt game. But I wasn't even on the bench. That's probably where all the trouble started between Jack and myself out there. I felt I was fit, he said I wasn't. But then I wasn't getting in the team and was getting a lot of niggling injuries. I still got to USA '94 but I hardly played in the last four or five years, which was unfortunate.

'I was still there or thereabouts in the squad. I captained the team in Liechtenstein. It was 0–0, which wasn't a very good result. I think we then played Austria at home and got stuffed by Austria in Dublin. I felt I played all right in that game but Jack came out in the papers afterwards and said we didn't have any legs in midfield. That was really the end of it. I was 34 or so and I wasn't going to go on much longer anyway. But it does come to a pretty abrupt end. You're not in the next squad and that's it. Nobody phones you to say you won't be playing again. It does just go like that. You feel it for a while that it might be coming. But when it happens it's very abrupt and that's the end of it. You're out of the squad and you're finished playing for Ireland.'

The story of Ronnie Whelan is linked with the years from 1981 to 1995, when the Republic of Ireland international side was transformed from also-rans into genuine contenders in world soccer. Side by side was his contribution to the extraordinary success of Liverpool in the 1980s. In such exalted company, his role is sometimes overlooked or forgotten. Yet at Anfield he is fondly recalled for his distribution, tackling, vision, consistency, reliability and his goal-scoring prowess. That he contributed enormously to the teams he played with is beyond dispute. That he did so at such a high level in domestic and European soccer perhaps defines his ultimate achievement.

'I feel very fortunate,' Ronnie concludes regarding his time with Liverpool. 'I look at it as three different teams. There was the one I came into with Souness and Dalglish. Then I went into a different one with Jan Molby, Kevin MacDonald in midfield and Steve McMahon. The last one was the Barnes, Beardsley, Aldridge and Houghton era. I felt I played with three very different teams but three very good teams. And I felt fortunate that I was there long enough to be part of all that happened in the '80s. The '90s weren't too good. But I tend to look back on the good times in the '80s.

'That team in the mid-1980s I felt could beat anybody. As a professional, the European Cup victory in Rome was a great memory. You go to Rome, playing Roma in their backyard. Nobody expected us to beat them; they had a very good side. It was one of the only times that I played for Liverpool in the 1980s when we were the underdogs in a game. Falcão played for Roma that day, Graziani, Conti; it was a great team they had. But from a personal point of view the highlight was lifting the FA Cup in '89. As a kid I was up at 10 o'clock on Saturday morning to watch the build-up throughout the day. I watched it completely to the end and watched whoever went up to pick the Cup up. As a kid you'd think: "God, I'd love to do that." And I was fortunate enough to do it in '89.

'When I went over there in '79 little did I think I'd come away with six League Championships, a European Cup, League Cups and FA Cups. I really feel fortunate that I was part of it. I was very lucky up to '90 when it started to go wrong with injuries. You have to be lucky. You have to be in the right place at the right time as a footballer. I've known better players than me that haven't won anything. But I was fortunate to be in Liverpool in the '80s and I thank God for that.'

15. PACKIE BONNER

IT WAS UNDOUBTEDLY THE MOST IMPORTANT SAVE IN THE HISTORY OF IRISH FOOTBALL.
Packie Bonner crouched like a cat on the line. Daniel Timofte
advanced. Silence enveloped the Luigi Ferraris Stadium in Genoa.
Pubs throughout Ireland fell silent. TV viewers turned their backs,
unable to watch. People embraced, consumed with tension. The
nation's streets were deserted. Bonner lunged to his right. His lips
were pursed. His eyes were focused. His face was a study in
concentration. His gloved hands stretched for the ball. He parried
the shot. He then pounded his fists in the ground with relief and joy.

Four times Bonner had failed to deny the Romanians. First there
was Hagi. Then there was Lupu. Next came Rotariu and Lupescu.
Each time Bonner dived the right way. Each time the ball ended up in
the net. On the fifth occasion Daniel Timofte wasn't so lucky. Next up
came David O'Leary. He struck the ball. The Romanian keeper was
left clutching air. A crescendo of noise filled the stadium. Irish living-
rooms erupted. Car horns blared. Pubs exploded with sound. People
converged on Dublin city centre. Flags were everywhere. Plans were
hatched for trips to Rome. As with the assassination of John F.
Kennedy or the World Trade Center atrocity of September 11, most
people can recall where they were at the moment when the Republic
of Ireland reached the quarter-finals of the 1990 World Cup.

'Up to that point I hadn't really done very much in the competition,'
Packie Bonner remembers. 'Before that, there wasn't much happening
as far as the goalkeeping side was concerned. I had to do something to
earn my corn and in the game against Romania I thought I played very
well. I kept a few shots out from Hagi and I was on a high because I
had done well. Suddenly this game was giving me what I wanted,
which was to go out to the World Cup and achieve.

'The penalty thing was an added bonus. I've always said that the goalkeeper isn't the one who is under pressure when it comes to this situation. I'd gone through the experience with Celtic about a month before in a penalty shootout. We had lost the Cup final after it going to 9–8. I think I went the wrong way for about five penalties. So I had to really do my homework.

'I spoke to Gerry Peyton a lot over the weeks leading up to the penalty shootout and he gave me good advice. The great thing about a penalty shootout is that you don't have to actually catch the ball. You don't have to knock it away to safety. You just have to keep it out of the goal and that's exactly what I did. But I was on a high. I felt that I could spring anywhere in the goal. Some days you're like that. Other days you're not.

'Luckily I went the right way for most of the penalties. The penalty that Daniel Timofte took wasn't a great penalty. It was an ideal height for a goalkeeper. He didn't go up to it very decisively. He always looked under pressure. Maybe I kind of psyched him out. I had talked to Gerry about the sort of run-up to the ball various players make. And it worked, to be honest. He ran up at a very acute angle and put it back into the same side that he was standing on. We had worked that out, and it worked for us.

'The reaction was incredible. To think that it could capture the imagination of the Irish public the way it did was remarkable. Young and old, men and women, people who probably were very traditional Gaelic people just got caught up in the whole thing. It became more than a game of soccer; it became a sort of national thing and we were all proud to be part of it.

'Everybody got involved in the celebrations, so it wasn't just the players out in Italy and the fans that went out there. We got great feedback from RTÉ. They sent out the tapes and we watched all the things that were happening around the country. That in itself spurred us on to make it last for as long as possible. We missed out on the parties in Ireland, there's no doubt. Everybody had barbecues and people were setting up plans for the next barbecue. So while we were under pressure in Italy, everybody was enjoying the celebrations in Ireland. The unfortunate thing was that you couldn't be in both places at the same time.'

In 1978 Packie Bonner left Keadue Rovers and County Donegal to join Glasgow Celtic. Spotted by Celtic's legendary scout Seán Fallon, he became Jock Stein's last signing before his dismissal as Celtic manager. At the time of Packie's arrival at Parkhead, Celtic were entering a moderately successful phase in their history. Rangers were sinking into a decade-long trough. Remarkably, Aberdeen and Dundee United were making claims to soccer prominence. Into that maelstrom of Scottish soccer stepped the young Packie Bonner.

Throughout the 1980s Packie shared in Glasgow Celtic's successes in Scottish domestic competitions. After effectively taking over in goal in 1980, he won Scottish League Championships in 1981, 1982, 1986 and 1988. He also shared in the club's Scottish FA Cup and Scottish League Cup victories. By any standards it was a relatively impressive haul of silverware, although inevitably the team were compared unfavourably to the great European Cup-winning Glasgow Celtic side of 1967.

'Seán Fallon came over to watch some games,' Packie recalls of his move from Donegal to Celtic. 'He obviously had been told about me before. He asked me over for trials and I went over in November 1977. Everything was snowed out. I think I played one game and Frank Connor, who was in charge of the reserves and who was an ex-goalkeeper with Celtic, came along and liked what he saw. He gave me a good report.

'I went back home. I was doing my Leaving Cert. at the time and I thought I didn't really have much chance. But I got a phone call near Easter to ask me to go over and play for Celtic in a tournament out in France. I went back and played and I really thought I had a very poor tournament indeed. I went back home and I thought: "That's definitely it, there's no chance of me ever getting a contract."

'Suddenly I got a phone call in May to say that the great Jock Stein himself was coming over and wanted to sign me. The nerves were tingling with the excitement. Myself and my dad and mum went out to Letterkenny to a hotel and there we met Jock Stein. I signed. I didn't care what I signed for. I think I got £70 a week, which was a good wage at that time. I signed for two years and I think he gave me £1,000 as a signing-on fee and he told me to look after my parents.

'I went over and I was lucky because I stayed with my uncle and aunt. In fact, I had two sets of aunts and uncles over there. I stayed with one for a while. When they moved back to Donegal, I went down the road and stayed with the other. I was lucky in that respect. I was well looked after. Unfortunately, my first aunt had sons and they were a lot older than me. In the other house they had a son and he was only a baby. So I really had nobody to hang around with from either family. I found that a real problem.

'I had left my family and friends back in Donegal. It was a traumatic experience. I remember going up to my room at night and saying: "What am I doing here?" I had a few tears in the eyes thinking about home. At the time we didn't have mobile phones. In fact, we didn't have a phone in our house in Donegal so it wasn't easy to keep in contact. I found that a really hard problem. It took me about two years to get over it. I was 18 at the time and I look back on it and I wonder how kids today are handling it when they go away at 14 or 15 years of age. They are maybe in bigger groups now. They're normally put into digs with three or four other guys and I think that does help. I didn't do that. I was secure but I was lonely.

'When I went on trial, Jock Stein and Seán Fallon, who was the chief scout, were there. They signed me and I joined Celtic in July and they were all gone. Jock was sort of given the door and Billy McNeill took over. Looking back on it, I would think it was probably good for me in one respect because Billy McNeill was making up his mind about everybody. He didn't have his favourites. He looked at the whole thing afresh. I made an impression, I suppose, because they sold Roy Baines, who was the second-choice goalkeeper. I was then the second choice. I made my début early in 1979. So I must have made some sort of impression, I suppose, for Billy to put me in the team so early.

'My first year on the team we won the Championship and my second year also. Aberdeen and Dundee United were a big challenge at the time. Rangers won nothing as far as the Championship was concerned in all that period right up to I think it was 1987. We could have won it six years on the trot. We threw it away against Dundee United and Aberdeen. Aberdeen had a very good team and they went on to win the European Cup Winners' Cup. They were an excellent team, but we were up there challenging.

'We didn't do anything in Europe and that was a big disappointment. We had beaten a very good Ajax team with Van Basten, Lerby and Olsen, all these guys in it. But we got knocked out in the next round against Real Sociedad. We were very disappointed because we felt that we could have done something that year. When you judge Celtic teams over time, they'll always be judged against the 1967 team. That's the unfortunate thing about it. You're always living that nightmare, that you're never as good as the 1967 team. But they were exceptional. We did OK, although the 1990s then became a bit of a disaster for us, no doubt about that.'

In 1981 Packie Bonner made his first appearance in a Republic of Ireland goalkeeper's jersey playing in the team's 3–0 defeat by Poland. The regular international goalkeeper at the time was Séamus McDonagh, with Packie and Gerry Peyton alternating in the back-up goalkeeping slot. It took until 1982 for Packie to win a second cap in the Republic's 2–0 loss to Algeria. A further year passed before he secured his third cap, although this time the result was a massive 8–0 victory over Malta. Indeed, it really wasn't until the arrival of Jack Charlton in 1986 that Packie became the regular goalkeeper for the Republic of Ireland team. From then on, he was a virtual ever-present in Jack's master plan.

'Eoin Hand was the manager who first picked me and he picked me really as a sub goalkeeper,' Packie recalls. 'Séamus McDonagh was the main goalkeeper and Eoin kind of swapped myself and Gerry Peyton around a little bit. I was a wee bit frustrated that I wasn't getting a chance in the team and I had only nine caps to my name when Jack took over. Looking back on it now, I was delighted in one respect because it gave me the opportunity to be part of the squad without being under severe pressure. I might have gone in as a young guy and been given a run with the team and not performed. That would have been the end of my international career.

'When Jack took over, I was 26 years old. I was at a right age and had good experience. I was strong mentally and things just happened for me after that. I made 71 caps between the age of 26 and the age of 35 or 36. So over a 10-year period I made most of my caps. I was in a good team under Jack and that helped the confidence also. When you look at the team when Jack started off, we had Mark Lawrenson and Liam Brady in it. We had a very big, strong team with Mick McCarthy, Kevin Moran, Paul McGrath, Dave O'Leary, Niall Quinn and Tony Cascarino. When you went out the tunnel and looked at the opposition, we were men compared to them. For a goalkeeper, that's a very satisfying thing.

'Jack also gave us a system to play and he made sure that you knew your role within that system. He pointed out to me in no uncertain terms that I had to become a bit of a sweeper. I did that already with Celtic. I played the game that way anyway. But we weren't the quickest at the back, especially in our centre-half positions, and I had to play the role of sweeper coming off my line and clearing things up.

'My thing in goalkeeping always had been that you stop the thing further up the pitch. Maybe there's a vulnerable side to me that I don't want to have to be called on to make a save because I may not be able to make it or take the cross or whatever. Get other guys up the pitch to do it. So I used my voice and I used to have Mick McCarthy in front of me and I would tell Mick whatever I wanted to get done. He would shout it. If there was somebody in midfield that wasn't in position and I had seen it, I told Mick and Mick did the shouting for me further up the pitch. It became a competition between myself and Mick as to who shouted the loudest. That was my way of keeping my concentration and I was dominant in that way.'

In 1988 Packie Bonner first laid claim to legendary status during Ireland's European Championship campaign. Through to a major tournament for the first time ever, virtually all the Irish players became household names overnight. No star, however, shone quite as brightly as Packie Bonner's, especially following the Republic's famous 1–0 victory over England at the Neckarstadion in Stuttgart. The England team was crammed with enormously skilful players like Hoddle, Waddle, Robson, Beardsley, Lineker and Barnes. Almost single-handedly, Bonner kept them at bay. On three occasions he denied Gary Lineker, who was through on goal, his final save a dramatic one in added time. It was, without doubt, the high point of Bonner's career.

'It was our first opportunity to play at a level that most of us had only dreamed about,' Packie reflects. 'To go out against England, who were traditionally our enemy as far as soccer was concerned, and to beat them 1–0 in Stuttgart, was a tremendous feat. We were under pressure for most of the game and especially later on when Glenn Hoddle came on the pitch. He was a great passer of the ball. Gary

Lineker was scoring goals right, left and centre at the time. So it was backs to the wall and I had to produce my best to keep them out. I'll never forget the emotional feeling when that final whistle went. Really we should have lost by about three or four goals in that game, but we didn't. I think it was probably one of the key moments in Jack's career as Ireland manager. We just grew in confidence after that.'

In 1990 Gary Lineker gained revenge on Packie Bonner with a depressingly ominous goal. The occasion was the Republic of Ireland's match with England in the World Cup finals in Cagliari. With England ahead from the early minutes, it seemed that the Republic's World Cup campaign might grind to a sudden halt. Fortunately, Kevin Sheedy made amends in the second half with an equaliser past Peter Shilton. Following further draws against Egypt and Holland, Ireland went through to the crucial next round of the 1990 World Cup finals.

'It was a huge game,' Packie recalls of that opening World Cup match against England. 'We were drawn against them again and they weren't looking forward to playing us because they knew how well we did against European teams. But it turned out to be very much a British-style game. The weather changed. It rained and the pitch wasn't that great. It became a typically dour English-type game that day. It wasn't for the people who loved the game of soccer. We drew the game after being a goal down, which was a break for us. We were lucky on the day.

'We went on then to play Egypt, which was a difficult game. People expected us to win that game quite easily, but they were difficult to break down. We got a lucky break against Holland. We hadn't won any games but we had qualified for the next round, which was a big thing to do. It was a World Cup, remember, and it was our first time in the World Cup. I think we had the whole nation behind us, and having a nation like Ireland behind you is a fantastic feeling.'

Few sporting events caught the public's imagination quite like the Republic of Ireland's World Cup campaign in 1990. 'Jack's Army' took Italy by storm. Savings accounts were raided to pay for trips to Cagliari, Palermo, Genoa and Rome. Workplaces came to a halt for Ireland's matches against England, Egypt, Holland, Romania and

Italy. Radio broadcasts and television screens were filled with images of the team's progress. It was a summer never to be forgotten by those old enough to witness the event. The homecoming summarised the national mood, with an estimated 300,000 to 400,000 people thronging the route from Dublin Airport to College Green. The people of Ireland appropriately paid tribute to their sporting heroes.

'Most of the guys came back to Ireland and enjoyed the homecoming so well,' Packie reflects. 'It was incredible flying in over Dublin and seeing thousands upon thousands of people thronging the airport and all the way into O'Connell Street. It was quite an incredible scene. But for me the best moment was going back home to Donegal. I didn't go back for a couple of days because I had to go back to Glasgow. I hadn't seen my wife and we had a new baby.

'Then we flew back into Carrickfin from Glasgow and there was a huge crowd down at Carrickfin waiting for me. There were bonfires everywhere. The bands were out. We stopped off at the Keadue pitch, we stopped off at Dungloe, we stopped off again down in Burtonport where there was a reception. It was an incredible thing. But it was everybody's moment too. It was my mum's moment. It was my brother's moment. It was my family's moment. It was about all the people that were back from Italy at this stage. It was their moment as much as mine, no question about that.'

As so often happens in football, just when it looks as if you can do no wrong, events turn against you. That's exactly what happened to Packie Bonner on 4 July 1994 at the Citrus Bowl in Orlando, Florida. Ireland's World Cup opponents were Holland. Needing a win to advance to the quarter-finals, disaster struck. An unfortunate back-header from Terry Phelan gifted Dennis Bergkamp a goal. Then, incredibly, Packie Bonner let Wim Jonk's seemingly straightforward long-range shot pass through his hands and into the net. Never was a reputation for steadiness and reliability so heavily tested than on that warm Florida day in July 1994.

'I did not enjoy the World Cup in the States,' Packie says. 'The most important reason was the professional reason that I didn't feel prepared mentally or physically. A goalkeeper needs to do his work during the week if he's to play. It's not like other players who put in 90 minutes of hard graft and then rest for two days before playing again in the next game. A goalkeeper might only have a little bit to do during a game so he has to do his preparation work during the week. You must get your mind right and your physical condition right to peak at certain times within the next game. I didn't achieve that in America.

'We trained down in Orlando. We went there to prepare, which looking back on it now might have been a mistake. You could train only for 20 minutes and you were absolutely gone. You were dehydrated. You just could not put in the work. Mentally I just did not feel that I was prepared. There's no doubt it affected my game because I made a horrendous mistake. Even in the Italy game, which we won, I just didn't feel right. I didn't feel that I was sufficiently at the top of my game to be going into a tournament of that magnitude.

'We all talk about the game against Holland in Orlando. I can't explain what happened. What I do know about it is that Wim Jonk got a ball about 30 yards out and the space opened up for him. He drove forward. It wasn't that hard a shot but it did move a little bit in the air. I took my eye off it. It was too easy. It happens to most goalkeepers at some stage but it's horrible to happen at that level, at that stage of a tournament, with the eyes of the world on you. But that's the way it goes. That's why goalkeepers are mad, they reckon. They have to go in there and perform and make the mistakes and then have to get back up and perform again afterwards. It's not easy to do it.

'The hardest part was trying to get over it. I was lucky that it was the last game of the season and I could go away for a holiday for the next three or four weeks. We also got a great reception when we came back home again to Ireland. I think that people forgave and forgave very quickly. People don't talk about it too much now and I'm glad they don't. They always talk about the Romanian save. It's nice to be remembered for the good things.'

By the time he retired from international football, Packie Bonner had won 80 caps playing for the Republic of Ireland. He also had won four Scottish League Championships, along with Scottish League Cups and Scottish FA Cups. More importantly, he had built a reputation as a powerful, agile, reliable keeper who dominated his area and was professional to the core. As a last-line sweeper in Jack Charlton's famous soccer teams from 1986 to 1995, his time in international football had tracked his manager's career almost precisely. In fact, although quite clearly a legend in his own right, it is as the last line of defence in Jack's famous sides that the name of Packie Bonner will forever be recalled.

'I'm glad I was around for the special time under Jack,' Packie concludes. 'We didn't win anything. But to get to a World Cup quarter-final and to go through a career with 80 caps and to play in a European Championship, two World Cups, with Celtic in League Championships and Cup finals, with the travel all over the world, it was unbelievable. People say: "If you were 10 years younger and you were just going through your career now, look at all the money you could earn." But I wouldn't change anything for all the money. I might be a little bit wealthier. But money can't buy you that feeling of happiness and success that I seemed to achieve.

'Nobody will forget it. People our age won't forget it and the people that are now in their 20s won't forget it. What's even strange for me is that there are kids out there at the age of maybe six or seven who know me by name. I've never met them in my life. Whether that's down to the parents or whether they're watching the videos, I don't know. Whether the name Packie has a trigger there for kids to remember it, again I don't know. But the kids do remember, although there's a lot who don't. I'm glad they don't, to be honest, because there's a new generation of footballers coming up now and the greatest satisfaction I would get is that another Irish team qualifies and plays in the World Cup. I want to be enjoying the barbecues here in Ireland, for a change.'

16. DAVID O'LEARY

TAKING A PENALTY IS THE ULTIMATE TEST OF A FOOTBALLER'S NERVE. FANS, PLAYERS, managers, cameras are focused primarily on you. Team dynamics are redundant. You are on your own. It's down to a battle of wits between you and the keeper. It's a high-pressure moment. The outcome of the game is often at stake. Making your mind up, picking the spot, judging your adversary's reactions, staying calm and collected are vital. Skill, technique and confidence are required. Then there is luck, which is often defined by the thickness of a crossbar, the condition of a boot or the size of a divot. Score and you're remembered forever. Miss and you're tarnished goods. Make no mistake but taking a penalty is a risky affair.

If you want to know about the pressures of penalty-taking, ask David O'Leary. It wasn't that he took them on a regular basis. In fact, he wasn't a penalty-taker at all. It was just that in June 1990 he scored the most important spot-kick in the history of Irish soccer. The setting was daunting. It was the end of a penalty shootout with Romania in the World Cup finals. A place in the quarter-finals was on offer. The atmosphere was intimidating. Packie Bonner had just saved from Daniel Timofte. Now David O'Leary stepped forward to make history. As the annals of Irish soccer show, he scored, calming a nation's ragged nerves as the Republic of Ireland reached heights never dreamed of before.

'I think a lot of people were surprised that I took the penalty,' David says. 'When I walked up I saw these thousands upon thousands of people in green behind the goal. You're on the halfway line. You walk out and the lads wish you all the best. I remember Kevin Sheedy's words: "Don't change your mind." As I walked up that long walk from the halfway line I said: "I'm going to put it to the goalkeeper's left. I'm going to get the ball off the referee. I'm just going to put it down on the spot and step back, run up and hit it to his left."

'I got the ball off the referee. I put it down. The referee was fussy and wanted it spotted again. I stepped back and I saw this wall of green that was so still at the back of the goal. I ran up and slotted it to the goalkeeper's left-hand side. Thank God he dived to the right. The ball hit the net. There was this unbelievable eruption of green and white behind the goal. My biggest mistake was standing still because I nearly got killed from the rush of all the players. Jack came up to me afterwards and said: "Well done, I knew you wouldn't miss." And he just walked away. But it was a fantastic feeling. I was delighted for the country, for the rest of the squad and I was delighted for myself.

'I always thought I would have loved to have played an individual game. Soccer is a brilliant game but no matter how much you prepare yourself, you're relying on the 10 other people. Have they looked after themselves right all week building up to the match? Have they trained right? Have they conducted themselves right afterwards? But when you're in an individual sport like golf, it's all about how you prepare yourself. I'm a golf fan and I've often thought that in soccer you never really get tested. I mean can you produce this 10-foot putt to win the Masters or the US Open with everybody watching you?

'I can remember Ian Woosnam at the Masters. He had this putt and if he put it in he'd win it. The whole world was watching. I thought I'd never get that in soccer. But I did in a round about way with a penalty to put my country through to the next round. I always felt I'd love to test myself to see could I put myself in that situation. And it fell to me. I knew I was up to it but I had to go and prove it.

'I haven't watched the penalty for 10 years at least. I know it's a long time ago but when you do watch the video it brings back great feelings. I remember my grandmother that time was in hospital. We were hearing the stories in Italy of how everybody was going crazy in Ireland. But the grandmother was a lady I loved very much. She was in there, in hospital, and she kept saying: "That's my grandson there." The nurse was probably thinking: "This old dear is doolally!" But I remember going up to the hospital after I got back and the nurses looked in amazement. I think they thought: "Oh, that old dear wasn't doolally in any way." I was delighted for her. I was delighted for my parents. And I was delighted to do it for my country as well.'

In terms of maturity alone, no one was better equipped to take that famous penalty in June 1990 than David O'Leary. He was, at the time, aged 32. With Arsenal he had tasted success in the League Championship, FA Cup and League Cup. He had played at the highest levels in Europe, including participating in a nail-biting European Cup Winners' Cup final. Just as importantly, he was rated as one of the finest defenders in world soccer – tall, composed, elegant, with great vision and a fine reader of the game. He was coolness personified, controlled, unflappable and recognised as such by his peers.

On the international stage, things weren't quite so rosy. Way back in 1976 David had made his Republic of Ireland début with a fine performance against England at Wembley Stadium. Slotting in alongside the likes of Giles, Brady, Givens, Mulligan, Daly and Heighway, the team gave a sterling performance in their 1–1 draw with the old enemy. A succession of appearances in qualifiers for European Championships and World Cups followed. By the time Jack Charlton took over in 1986, David was a virtual ever-present in the side.

Unfortunately, O'Leary's central role with the Republic of Ireland changed abruptly in the wake of Jack Charlton's accession to office. Following a controversial falling-out with the manager over his unavailability for the Iceland tournament in May 1986, he was effectively banished from the squad. Controversy ensued, with David's many admirers and supporters clamouring for his reinstatement. With the manager unmoved, it took many years in the wilderness before he was restored to the team. How ironic it was then that David O'Leary should come on as a sub against Romania in 1990 to score perhaps the most crucial goal in Irish soccer history!

'First of all, I thought Jack Charlton did a fantastic job for Ireland,' David remarks. 'He was good for Ireland and Ireland was good for him. They both got the best out of it. But was I treated unfairly by Jack Charlton? Yes, unbelievably. I was disappointed with a lot of people in Ireland who wanted to go along under the Jack banner, didn't want to upset him, didn't want to speak out. I'll always remember those people. But I was left out of the Iceland trip and because other people pulled out I was called back in. In that time, when I'd been left out, I had made other arrangements to do something. I couldn't rearrange them. Other people pulled out who didn't fancy going to Iceland. And I was the one that was made a scapegoat for it really.

'I don't feel bitter about it. I think Jack made a big mistake. He'll never admit it. But he was big enough and man enough to call me back about three years later. I probably played the best football of my career in those three years. Whether that was because I wasn't playing international football I don't know. But I certainly missed international football. I was one of the few lads whose family lived in Ireland. My family had to live with three years of: "When will O'Leary ever play?" When I did get back and played I was so proud for my mum and dad, who were so disgusted by the way I'd been treated and missed my going over and representing my country. And I think the icing on the cake was scoring the penalty against Romania because that was a brilliant thing.'

Back in the 1970s the rhythmical recitation of 'Brady-Stapleton-O'Leary' rolled easily off everyone's lips. Although it's often presumed that all three players arrived at Highbury together, the truth is that Brady and Stapleton were already there when the young David O'Leary turned up with his suitcases. Aged 15 he arrived in London at the same time as another young hopeful named John Murphy. Murphy would soon succumb to homesickness and return to Ireland, where he forged a name for himself in international rugby. David O'Leary, however, who was a former schoolboy footballer with Shelbourne, stuck it out. Having joined as an apprentice in 1973, he steadily rose through the ranks and made his first-team début in 1975. He was aged 17 at the time.

'John Murphy and myself came across and Stapleton and Brady were there,' David recalls. 'There was a kind of pulling thing. You had two Irish lads there, who were making good names for themselves. We were the babies that came underneath them. It was nice to have lads from Dublin there to help you. John Murphy went back with homesickness. I wasn't too far behind him, greatly missing Dublin and the family. Then John Devine came. He had great potential as well and got into the team. You had Sammy Nelson and Pat Rice there, who were great. They were very influential people. Pat Jennings came on the back of that. So Arsenal, through no intention of their own, was starting to build up a right Irish mafia.

'The first year I thought was a bit of a disaster. I was homesick and I didn't play particularly well. Towards the last half-dozen games, the training and the adapting to a new way of life were coming together. I went home that summer, came back after six weeks and was homesick again. But I got put into the reserve side and had a very good season in the reserves. At the start of the following season, my third season there, I had just turned 17 and I got picked for the first team to go to Scotland on tour. Then I got picked for the first League game. It was fantastic.

'It was a big club at the time. We all heard about the Double-winning side. But Arsenal were changing. They wanted to get new people in. The tradition, the set-up and the way they did things at the club was fantastic. The club was geared to be successful. It was geared as well for its great youth set-up. I signed for them mainly because you felt that if you did well there, they had such a great youth policy that they'd give you a chance to break through. It was very demanding and very good. If you were good enough, they were willing to give you a chance. And that's what we were all aiming for.

'The team started to have some tremendous youngsters come through. Brady was an exceptional player, who was probably as good as anybody I've ever played with. He was starting to emerge. Frank Stapleton was starting to blossom into a fantastic centre-forward. He was as good as you got. I was starting to come through and people were starting to say nice things about me. Pat Jennings arrived. He was a keeper that Tottenham decided wasn't good enough. He came across to the arch-enemy and he was still a world-class goalkeeper. We had two solid full-backs in Rice and Nelson. The team was really starting to take shape. It was an exciting time, an exciting place to be, with exciting players and we were playing some exciting football. They were great times, happy times.'

It wasn't until well into the second half of the 1970s that Arsenal shed the baggage of the Double-winning success of '71. Like all great teams, that historic side took a while to break up. In time, players like Bob Wilson, Frank McLintock, Ray Kennedy, Charlie George,

John Radford, George Armstrong and Peter Simpson moved on. Arsenal's manager Bertie Mee moved on too. Replaced in 1976 by Terry Neill, the club blossomed once more. Three FA Cup finals in succession followed. Two defeats – to Ipswich in 1978 and to West Ham in 1980 – are best forgotten. Victory over Manchester United in 1979 was another story indeed. Six Irishmen played in that match – Jennings, Rice and Nelson from Northern Ireland and Brady, Stapleton and O'Leary from the Republic of Ireland. That day, aged 21, David O'Leary tasted his first major success.

'It was an amazing adventure,' David says. 'Growing up as a kid in Dublin you'd watch the FA Cup final and think what a brilliant occasion it was. Then to get to one was unbelievable, even though the Ipswich game proved a disaster. We were beaten 1–0 and should have been beaten by more. People said: "You're lucky to get to one Cup final in your career." I thought: "Well, we've been beaten in that and God knows when we'll ever get back."

'We got back the following year and we played Manchester United. It was the dream match: north versus south, the two biggest clubs in the country. And we won. It was fantastic because of what we'd gone through the year before. When the referee blew the whistle, it was great to know you had won the game and all your family was there. I remember going back to Dublin that summer with the medal and saying I'd played in a Cup-winning team against Manchester United. It was a fantastic feeling for a lad coming from Dublin.'

Following the three FA Cup final appearances, Arsenal went into a period of decline for a large chunk of the 1980s. There was one last highlight in 1980 – the European Cup Winners' Cup final, which they lost to Valencia – before the rot set in. The run that ensued was awful, including a home defeat by Walsall in the League Cup in 1983 and a loss to York City in the FA Cup in 1985. It was hard to believe that a club of Arsenal's stature could sink so low.

Although David played in both those games, he also was there for the club's revival of fortunes as the 1980s came to a close. Having come fourth and sixth in the League in 1987 and 1988 respectively, Arsenal produced one last amazing flourish as the decade ended. In 1989, in a famous showdown at Anfield, they grabbed the League title from under Liverpool's nose. In the depths of added time

Michael Thomas scored the crucial goal that denied Liverpool and brought the Championship to Highbury. It was an extraordinary climax to the season, with Arsenal securing the Championship and David O'Leary winning a prized League medal.

'Arsenal had won in '71 and hadn't done it since,' David recalls. 'I'd been at the club since '73 and all you heard was the same old story. Then it was great to go to a place like Anfield and win it. For us needing to win by two clear goals and to have to win the League against the best side over the last 10 years was a one-off, memorable experience. I don't think TV did justice to it. It was like a Cup final although it was for the League title. And for Michael Thomas to score the way he did in injury-time was phenomenal. It was an unbelievable feeling to win your first League Championship with Arsenal. It was really fantastic.

'It was an incredible week in many ways. After the Anfield game I was faced with two games to help secure us to go to the World Cup in Italy. I remember it was a Friday evening and I was coming over to Dublin on the Saturday to play for Ireland on the Sunday. We faced games against Malta and then Hungary the following week. So in the space of a week you could win the League and if you won the two games at home you could maybe set yourself up to go to a World Cup. We won all three of the games. I remember finishing at the end of the following week thinking: "That's been a fantastic week."'

As the 1990s began, David O'Leary was still appearing with the Arsenal first team although less frequently than in earlier years. He helped the club secure another League title in 1991. He also won what was his second League Cup in 1993. Now well into his 30s, he broke all the club's records by chalking up an incredible 722 appearances. In a career spanning 20 years he had won all the major domestic trophies although success in Europe proved elusive. Fittingly, his time with the Gunners came to a close in the 1993 FA Cup final replay against Sheffield Wednesday. That day in May 1993 he walked off the Wembley turf with another FA Cup medal.

'I always thought going over as a Dublin lad that the more you were there at the place the more you'd want to stay,' David remarks. 'I always thought I wanted to do at least 10 years at the place and win things in that time. Then you got to 10 years and everybody thought you were a lot older because you had been playing for that long. I thought I wanted to play until I was 35 there. I wanted to do exactly 20 years there. I didn't say it out loud. I just had the personal ambition that I wanted to win everything I could with them and wanted to break the appearance record and see could I get to 35 while playing. I had joined in '73 and if I could get to '93 it would be 20 years.

'If Arsenal had released me the year before, after 19 years, people would have said: "Brilliant, he's lasted 19 years there." But they wouldn't have known that I wanted to stay and achieve a personal record of 20 years there. When I broke the George Armstrong record of 600-odd games, I wanted to be the first Arsenal player to go on to the 700s and have nobody else do it. I thought: "Yeah, I'm grateful to beat that great player George Armstrong but I want to be the first Arsenal player to go on to the 700s." That was even better for me, breaking that. It was a great, personal thing to get to '93 and do 20 years there. And the icing on the cake in that May, when I was 20 years at the club, was that I was in a Cup final.

'I can't believe how it happened because it was the Cup final against Sheffield Wednesday. What a way to finish! To go around Wembley carrying the trophy was a sad and a fantastic way to go. I knew once I got right around the pitch and into the tunnel that it would be the last game I'd play for Arsenal. But I thought that after 20 years it was a memorable way to finish, a great way and maybe it was the right way.'

Although David O'Leary went on to play for and manage other clubs, he never lost his association with Arsenal where, to this day, he is regarded as one of the London side's greatest legends. The respect with which he is held at Arsenal is hardly surprising given the length of his stay and the loyalty he showed to the club and its fans. In his time with the Gunners he displayed grace under pressure and showed himself to be an intelligent reader of the game. While no one doubted his class, he also had the nerve, steel and character to survive even the toughest of encounters. For his contribution to the Londoners he will long be remembered.

From an Irish perspective, David O'Leary's legacy is different. Images remain of his controversial exclusion from the squad under Jack Charlton's managerial reign, thus restricting the number of caps he received to a total of 68. There are other images as well, especially of the grace and style he displayed in a Republic of Ireland shirt. But no image can surpass that summer's day in June 1990 when he stepped up to propel that historic, match-winning penalty to the back of the Romanian net. It was to prove an enduring and defining moment in a wonderful football career.

'I always thought I was capable of doing 100 caps for Ireland,' David concludes. 'I always wanted to do it. I thought I was denied that. I'd love to have done that from a personal point of view. To be out for three years and in those three years probably to play the best football of your career was a big disappointment personally. But for a lad coming over in '73 and homesick for the first couple of years, if somebody had said in '73 that I'd still be in England today, still in football, still making a decent name, I'd have probably had them locked up.

'I still support Arsenal. I think since I've left them they've become even a bigger and better club. I always look out for their results and I always want them to do well. They sent me a video of their history and it was fantastic to play a big part in it. I was a lad coming over from Dublin at 15 thinking: "I wonder will I last a year or a couple of years there?" And they now say: "This lad from Dublin lasted 20 years there and he's remembered for it." I'm very proud as a lad from Dublin doing that. I'm proud to come from Dublin and to keep putting Dublin and Ireland on the map and trying to make people at home proud. I'm a very lucky person. Life's been good to me. God's been good to me. And long may it continue.'

17. PAUL McGRATH

TWO GREAT MATCHES IN ROME AND NEW JERSEY MARKED THE HIGH POINTS OF PAUL
McGrath's football career. The games were in majestic venues –
Rome's Olympic Stadium and New Jersey's Giants Stadium. With
Italy providing the opposition on both occasions, the atmosphere
was electric. The tournaments were the ultimate in soccer – the
World Cup finals of 1990 and 1994. The stakes were high. Media
coverage was worldwide. There was no better opportunity for great
players to raise their game, to display their skills, to take on the best,
to grab the moment against world-class talent. Paul McGrath rose to
the challenge on both occasions.

Ireland's Black Pearl was immense in the battles with Italy. He
excelled in Rome. In New Jersey he went one better. In both cases he
was facing quality opponents. Baresi, Maldini, Donadoni and
Roberto Baggio played in both matches. Dino Baggio played in New
Jersey. Schillaci, Costacurta, Albertini and Signori figured in one or
other of the games. They were all great players. Against them Paul
McGrath displayed skills that were close to perfection.

Both were colourful occasions involving passionate fans. Giants
Stadium was awash with Irish banners and flags. Some 30,000 Irish
supporters secured tickets for the match. Vastly outnumbering the
Italians, they inspired their team to a famous 1–0 victory. Four years
previously an estimated 20,000 Irish fans travelled to Rome, many
borrowing from banks and credit unions to pay for their trips. On
that occasion, following Schillaci's goal, they returned empty-
handed. They were wonderful events – proud, intense, emotional,
defining moments that unified the country as never before. Those
games, Paul McGrath claims, were his finest moments.

'Definitely the greatest game for me was at Giants Stadium,' Paul says. 'Everything went right on the day. We scored through Ray Houghton. To hang on as we did was great. It wasn't just a case of hanging on; I think we played some good football that day as well. And we got a result. I'll always remember walking out on the pitch for the start of that game and looking around and seeing that the place was Irish. There wasn't that much blue and there were lots of green shirts about. It made the hair stand up on the back of your neck.

'Both of the Italy games stood out for me. In Italia '90 it was unreal to walk out on that pitch and to see the Irish supporters. Italia '90, with it being the World Cup, with us getting as far as we did in that competition and then to play Italy in Rome, and the way everything seemed to come together with the Irish supporters, it was just like a month-long party and it was an incredible experience. I know for a fact that none of the lads that were involved will ever forget how the supporters made us feel. As players we had the easy job of going out there and enjoying something that we loved doing. But the reaction that the Italians got from the Irish people going there and showing how to enjoy a competition, without trouble as well, was something else.'

It all began so differently for Paul McGrath back in 1959. Far from the glamour of World Cups and professional football, he was born in sad circumstances three weeks before Christmas at the close of the decade. His mother, who was unmarried, gave birth to her son in a hospital in North London. The baby boy was quickly returned to Dublin, where he was brought up first in foster care and later in orphanages. Football was the love of his life, the vehicle for self-expression and, ultimately, the means of escape. Playing with Pearse Rovers, Dalkey United and St Patrick's Athletic, he excelled at the game. English clubs came knocking. Only one, Manchester United, got a positive response. This was the era of Ron Atkinson, the brash, charismatic manager whose teams always played stylish football and whose players were class acts. The Manchester club's offer of a month's trial was irresistible.

'As soon as I walked into Ron Atkinson's office the one thing he noticed more than anything was that I wore an earring,' Paul recalls of his introduction to Old Trafford in early 1982. 'He said to me: "If we're going to buy you, the one thing we don't want is centre-halves with earrings." I said: "Oh, it comes out." Kevin Moran said it was because he had all the jewellery and he was a bit put back that I had some of it. But he was a great manager. He was just a larger-than-life character. I loved him. I really did like him because it was really a fun club with him.

'The one thing I found difficult was the training. At St Pat's we trained twice in the week. To suddenly go from that to training every day was very difficult. I eventually got the hang of it and was able to keep up. Initially, though, I played a few games and they went really well. I was still very nervous about whether they'd keep me or not. But they did. At the end they said: "We want to keep you."

'It was great for me to be involved with the likes of Bryan Robson and Ray Wilkins, people I admired. The big thing for me was that Frank Stapleton was there. Kevin Moran was there. Ashley Grimes was there. There was a great splattering of Irish there, which helped enormously. That was really good. From that point of view I just fitted in straight away.'

Paul McGrath made his first-team début at the start of the 1982–83 season in a charity-match at Aldershot. His next appearance was in a League Cup contest with Bradford. It was only a matter of time before he made his League début. The moment finally arrived in November 1982 when he lined out against Spurs. With Gordon McQueen and Kevin Moran established as the club's centre-halves, it was hard to secure regular selection. However, Paul chalked up a solid run of first-team appearances that season. He also was a squad member when Manchester United won the FA Cup in 1983, although he failed to make it either into the side or onto the bench. FA Cup success would have to wait until 1985, when Paul partnered Kevin Moran at the heart of defence. However, the League title proved elusive, which was something that cost Ron Atkinson his job in November 1986.

'The League was the Holy Grail as far as the fans were concerned,' Paul reflects. 'We had a very talented team. The players we had back then included Norman Whiteside, Kevin Moran, Bryan Robson, Ray Wilkins, Jesper Olsen. There was a lot of talent around. But we always under-achieved, which was a shame. I think we went close a couple of times but we never actually won the thing. It did weigh on our shoulders that we were never going to make the grade. That was always in the background. We always had fabulous support and it was worrying that we weren't doing enough to bring home the League Championship.'

Throughout his years with Manchester United, Paul McGrath's career was already being overshadowed by problems with his dodgy knees. The first intimation of trouble came in the final reserve-team game of his first season, when a bad tackle resulted in surgery. The following years were filled with references to orthoscopes, cartilage tissue, knee-cleaning procedures, major surgery and intensive physical rehabilitation. A succession of operations ensued. Speculation focused on the extent of the damage. There were reports of flaking of the bone. The physical pain was exceeded only by worries concerning Paul's future in football. In truth, Paul McGrath's injuries became something of a national obsession, with media commentators and the sporting public intrigued by Irish soccer's most notorious knees.

'I honestly think that the change from training twice a week back in Ireland for an hour or maybe an hour and a half to going into professional football was very difficult,' Paul remarks regarding his knee problems. 'Putting your body under the sort of strain that I put it under when I first started with Manchester United, training every day and as hard as we trained, was difficult. The first season I played with them, they were going away on a tour to Canada. I made it on the panel to go away. Then I got injured in the last reserve game of the season against Sheffield United. I missed out on the trip. I had to have my knee done then. That was the first operation I had on my right knee.

'I had never been injured in my life over in Ireland. I only had the one pair of boots with St Pat's and never had an injury. When I went to Manchester United I bought a couple of pairs of boots and thought: "Here I am, I've arrived." Then my first injury came. Everything was going so well. Suddenly, getting that injury I thought: "Maybe it's not going to happen for me." I couldn't break into the first team. I was trying to get back as quick as possible because I wanted to break into the first team and I wanted everything to be right. You then start pushing yourself harder and harder. You demand certain things from your body when the body is trying to tell you to slow down a bit. But I persevered and got the head down and got my knee straight again. Luckily, the second season I got a few games and started to break into the team.

'Then I kept slipping back. As a professional footballer you can't afford to pull out of challenges, which I never wanted to do anyway. So the injuries seemed to pile up on me. They were always bad enough for me to have an operation. That was the worst thing about it. A lot of lads had hamstring injuries and strains and stuff, where you really need rest. Unfortunately, mine always seemed to be ones where I had to go under the knife. My knees, in particular, were a big problem with me in my time with Manchester United.'

Side by side with Paul's knee problems came controversy over the player's lifestyle while on the staff at Manchester United. The issue came to a peak following the arrival of new manager Alex Ferguson in 1986. Although an admirer of Paul's talents as a footballer, Ferguson was little impressed with the club's drinking culture, which was a problem he set about rectifying soon after his accession to office. Along with Norman Whiteside, Paul was a target for disciplinary action. He was fined for drinking and being late for training. Speculation mounted that the relationship between manager and player was unsustainable. It got particularly bitter following an allegedly tipsy appearance by Whiteside and McGrath on television prior to a Cup game against QPR. The net result was Paul McGrath's departure from Manchester United in the summer of 1989.

'Norman and myself were the younger people in the crew and we did get a reputation for sinking a few beers,' Paul remarks. 'But as regards the bad-boy image, we weren't bad boys at all. I used to fall asleep when I had too many to drink. Norman just loved a drink; it was as simple as that. But there was Bryan and Kevin who always made sure we didn't misbehave or anything like that. There was none of that sort of stuff. It was just young lads acting a little bit crazy at times, acting daft because we felt we were just having a couple of pints and we were going to enjoy ourselves and that's it.

'Initially that was when we were both injured. It's a depressing time for any professional when you're injured. You see all the other boys going into training. You're kind of put to one side because you're doing a different fitness regime to them. Norman and myself were injured quite a lot together. Norman had his fair share of injuries as well. We were in digs together. We found we had a lot of time on our hands. We'd do our stint in the morning with Jim McGregor, the physio. Then we'd say to each other: "Do you fancy going out for a couple of pints?" And we did go out once or twice into town and really sink a few. It crept up on us until all of a sudden we realised that they were all talking about us. We had this bad-boy image.

'Alex just had enough of it. Norman used to be in Alex's office and Alex would be giving him a dressing-down. Norman would be on the way out and I'd be on the way in. I'd be saying to him: "How much did you get fined this time?" And he'd be saying: "Oh, it's a big one this time." It was all a bit of a giggle for us. We were that daft at the time that we used to think that it was a bit of *craic*. We thought he was just going to slap us with a fine and it would all be forgotten.

'Alex Ferguson was well within his rights to let us both go. We did it on too regular a basis. We always believed that if we played and put it in for him on the football pitch then our private life should be whatever we wanted it to be, within reason. I genuinely did believe that I was playing well for Alex at the time. But, looking back, I can understand. Manchester United have an image to protect. They deserved more from me off the field and I wasn't giving it to them. It was as simple as that.

'When the end came I was up at Bryan Robson's house, at a barbecue, and a phone call came through on Bryan's phone. He said: "Paul, it's for you." I thought: "It's for me, in your house?" It was Alex and he said: "Graham Taylor has been on for you and I've said he can speak to you." And he just put the phone down. I thought: "Well, OK then." I spoke to Graham Taylor. As quick as lightning the deal was done and I was away to Villa Park.'

Having been signed by Graham Taylor for Aston Villa, Paul McGrath went on to demonstrate the same football skills that had won the fans' admiration at Old Trafford. He became a terrace favourite at Villa Park and was instrumental in the club's drive for the League title in the early 1990s. He won the League Cup in 1994 and 1996. Unfortunately, Aston Villa twice narrowly lost out in the Championship, to Liverpool in 1990 and to Manchester United in 1993. Those near misses were tragic for a player who was approaching the end of his career. By 1993 he was heading rapidly into his 30s and his injuries had escalated to frightening proportions. He was, quite literally, a walking wreck.

'My injuries became very severe in my time with Aston Villa,' Paul says. 'I could be out on the pitch doing a warm-up for a game and be feeling to myself that I physically wasn't going to be able to play the game. My knees were that sore that I would be wondering what I was doing even warming up for a game. But I believed that come 2.45 pm, when I came back from the warm-up, the adrenaline would kick in. Once it kicked in it would kind of take care of the pain. I don't know how that works but it actually did take care of the pain. The excitement of playing, or whatever, overcame the feeling of discomfort and pain that I got.

'I had a totally different training schedule to the rest of the lads. I didn't join in a lot of the hard running. I did in pre-season; I always joined in as much as I could there. But once the season started, the games took care of my fitness. I didn't train. I used to go up to the training-ground, I'd get in the bath, have a stretch. And, physically, I wouldn't exert myself very much during the week. Then I'd just play the games, get some rest and get ready for the next games. Villa were very good to me in that way and I'd like to think that I was there to repay them on the football pitch.

'It worked out that things went superbly for me there. People were giving me trophies for fun. But I genuinely think a lot of it was to do with the fact that we played a different system when I went there. There were players of great calibre beside me. I just cleaned up. It made it so simple for me with the dodgy knees. It really made it easy for me. And I enjoyed playing alongside the calibre of player that was there. They were tremendous. They knew I had certain problems with the running side of things. They really did try their best for me, to keep the movement I had to do down to a minimum.'

By the time Paul McGrath joined Aston Villa in 1989, he was already an established member of the Republic of Ireland squad. In fact, way back in 1985 he had made his first appearance for his country in a friendly against Italy at Dalymount Park. Injuries permitting, he continued to line out for the international side in the years ahead, sharing in the tournament success in Iceland in 1986, appearing in two of the three matches at Euro '88 and producing magnificent form at Italia '90. Although his skills were clearly evident at club level, he produced something extra on the bigger stage. Phrases like world-class were regularly used when describing McGrath's international prowess.

Alongside Paul's great displays, however, were some worryingly dark forces overshadowing his personal life and career. In the wake of Italia '90 his drinking got worse. He missed the European Championship qualifier against Turkey in October 1990 following a binge of giant proportions. He again went missing for the qualifier against Albania in the lead-up to the 1994 World Cup finals. The demons took over Paul's life. Crocked knees or not, his propensity to self-destruct was all too evident. Even Jack Charlton was driven demented by McGrath's erratic and unpredictable behaviour, although the manager was a great protector and admirer of the troubled star.

'He was great for Irish football and he was great to me,' Paul says of Jack Charlton. 'I was in the Irish set-up and when he took over he said to me: "I want you to play in the middle of the field." I was very disappointed. Then I'd look around the dressing-room and see the likes of Mark Lawrenson, Dave O'Leary, Kevin Moran, Mick McCarthy. We had a wealth of great centre-halves. I was happy to get in anywhere on a football pitch. I would have hoped it would be at centre-half. But when I looked at those players I couldn't argue. My all-time hero, anyway, was Liam Brady. So I thought that to be in the middle with Liam was a dream come true. The likes of Ronnie Whelan was in there as well.

'Jack explained to me the sort of job he wanted me to do, which was break up the play and basically throw my weight around if I could. He wanted me to be captain as well. He said to me: "Paul, I want you to take the ball out." I walked away and said: "Yes, no problem." It wasn't until I thought about it that I wondered: "What does he mean by 'take the ball out'?" When I went to Liam Brady and Frank Stapleton I said: "Jack has just asked me this and I do believe he's wanting me to be captain." With the likes of Frank Stapleton, Kevin Moran and Liam Brady in the side, I said: "Will you go and explain to him that I don't want to be captain." I wanted to be in the team and I wanted to be concentrating on what I was doing. It was a new role for me.

'Over the years he was magnificent to me. If ever I had a problem, Jack would come and sit down with me and thrash things out. He'd give me a bollocking from time to time. But he'd really be there to help me and get me sorted. Sometimes he'd look at me like he'd love to smash my head off something. I'd say I was a frustrating player to have managed. I genuinely don't do things to annoy people but I do annoy people. I know that for a fact. I don't do it for the reason that I want to get on people's bad side or get them angry with me. I genuinely don't. I'm sure there were loads of times Jack has looked at me and thought: "Is this worth it?" But he was a really decent man to me. At times when I've really felt low he's been so good to me. I owe him a lot. And there's a hell of a lot of games I played for Ireland that if somebody else was managing the team maybe I wouldn't have had the chance to play.'

In many ways, Paul McGrath's performances at USA '94 marked the final high points of his international football career. Encouraged by Jack Charlton, Paul somehow battled on to his last hurrah on the world stage. Following the tournament he continued to play with both club and country, eventually amassing a total of 83 caps. Then, having moved to Derby County and finally to Sheffield United, he retired in 1998, leaving the game with a coveted PFA Footballer of the Year award won in 1993. The Black Pearl, the man known to Aston Villa fans as God and the player affectionately immortalised in the terrace chant 'Ooh Aah Paul McGrath', had finally departed the scene.

'With Ireland, Jack was put out to grass, as they say, and Mick came in,' Paul concludes. 'It was a new era. I think Jack's only problem was that he kept faith with one or two of the older players because they had done so well for him. I was one of them. He wanted us to tell him when it was time for us to go. But a lot of us wouldn't tell him. We wanted to play on. I'd still like to play for Ireland. So Jack's only problem was that he let us go on a little bit too long and maybe should have cut our rein a little bit shorter.

'Mick was very honest with me and up-front. He brought me back for a few games. Things went very well for me at Derby and then I moved to Sheffield United. But footballers know when their time is up. I had my right knee operated on once more. I could tell when I went back training with them that it was never going to be the same. It was a really sad day for me when I had to quit with both Ireland and Sheffield United. It's like a bolt from the blue that really knocks you for six when you realise that the thing you loved doing for so long you weren't going to be able to do any more. It was a sad day. But I used to look back and think: "Everything that has happened to me is like a dream, being involved with Ireland across the world, hearing people chant your name." People only dream about that sort of stuff but I know that's actually happened to me. And I love the fact that I was able to represent Ireland in soccer. It's a dream come true for me.

'You couldn't have written the script. There are certain things that, obviously, I'd like to erase from the script. But I look back now and think: "That's something that happened to me, that was the way my path was to lead me." For the good times I've had it was well worth it to have the few bad times I've had as well. And I'd like to think, especially over the last couple of years anyway, that I've grown an awful lot. But I think I've been blessed. I honestly think that. I've been blessed to have had the career in soccer that I've had.'

18. NIALL QUINN

IT WAS ONE OF THOSE MAGIC MOMENTS AT LANSDOWNE ROAD. THE BALL WAS CROSSED to the far post, out of reach of the Cyprus defence. Niall Quinn stooped and headed it to the back of the net. In an instant, the stadium rose to its feet. Spectators burst into wild applause. They gave him a standing ovation. They sang 'Happy Birthday'. They waved banners, flags and scarves. The players converged on the Sunderland striker. The outpouring of affection was extraordinary to witness. It was, after all, a remarkable occasion. Aged 35 that day, Niall Quinn had just broken Frank Stapleton's 20-goal record. Although the Republic of Ireland team had qualified for a World Cup play-off and the chance of a trip to Japan and Korea, that evening in October 2001 belonged to only one player – the inevitable Man of the Match, Niall Quinn.

'The goodwill that descended on the ground at that moment was unbelievable,' Niall recalls of his 21st goal for the Republic of Ireland. 'I've scored goals before in big situations. I scored in a World Cup when I was a young and inexperienced player. But that night I got carried away a little bit with emotion. I did actually lose it for about five, six or seven seconds after I scored. It must be like the way pop stars feel when they've sung a song and the kids are screaming their heads off. It was a feeling that the moment was for me. The ball got kicked off and I ran around for a few seconds and I didn't even know if I was running in the right part of the pitch. I lost touch a bit.

'Afterwards, when you start to think about it you say: "I'm delighted for my mother and father." Everywhere they went people were saying: "Is that son of yours going to get the record?" My wife Gillian was getting it as well: "Is your husband ever going to get the record?" It even made its way to England. People would stop me in the street. That's the power of the media nowadays. The topic seemed to just fly and fly. I wouldn't call it pressure but I was getting funny stick, witty stick.

'The guys in the media were a little bit unfair because I missed the games against the easy lads with a back problem. I had a good chat with Mick McCarthy and Peter Reid about it, agreeing that I'd try to build myself up so that I was ready to play against Holland and Portugal while in the games against Andorra and Cyprus Mick wouldn't need me as much. If I really wanted the record that badly I'd probably have ditched the Holland and Portugal games and made sure I was fit and available for the other games. That's just a decision I made. It was a professional decision, which in the end caused me so much grief amongst the media lads. They turned around and said: "It's been so many months since Niall Quinn has scored." What they omitted to say was that in terms of 90 minutes of football it amounted to about two-and-a-half games because I'd been taken off early in so many matches and missed so many. They put a different slant on it and of course the pressure built up.

'I did feel, though, that the script had been written for me in the home match against Cyprus. It was my birthday. We needed goals. I had hit 35, which everyone seems to say is the footballer's pension age. It was do-or-die. It was a now-or-never kind of thing. I didn't feel pressure about it until I spoke to the missus before the game. I rang her before we left the hotel and she said: "Oh, really, this is the worst I've ever felt for you, ever, ever." And I said: "Why is that?" Then she explained to me how the script had been written and I had got to score. I thought: "Oh, my God." I hadn't thought of it like that. So I did feel a little bit of pressure then.

'Even though it was my birthday, I had been a bit reluctant to arrange any kind of party because if things didn't work out it would be the flattest birthday party of all time. I had never had a birthday party besides my 21st, which I had in a pub with about five people. So I wouldn't let Gillian arrange anything. We did say we'd go to a pub, to Kehoe's in South Anne Street, after the match. I thought we'd have five or ten people in for a drink. But what happened afterwards was just ridiculous. Every one of the players got wind of it and came in. To a man, every one of them came; even people like Clinton Morrison, who'd only known me a short time. They gave me a big "well done" and "happy birthday" and there was a huge cake. It was just a special night. Then we all made our way to a nightclub. All I know is that I left it in full flow and it was 7.45 in the morning.

'The next day I was at a junior football match down in Wicklow at one o'clock in the afternoon. The rain was something else. I've never seen rain like it. It was nice because I got away from the glitz and the glamour. I went down to my pal who manages a team and they lost. It was back down to earth, glum faces. The reality of sport is a wonderful thing. It keeps us all going. The contrasts that weekend were huge.'

In that World Cup qualifier against Cyprus in 2001, Niall Quinn was in the twilight of his distinguished football career. A long time had elapsed since the early 1980s when, at the age of 16, he played hurling for the Dublin minors. His team lost to Galway in the 1983 All-Ireland minor final. Offers of a career in Australian Rules football and an unsuccessful trial at Fulham were put in the shade by a trial at Arsenal. After scoring a hat-trick for the Arsenal U-18 team and performing impressively in a training-session with the first team, the offer of a contract was guaranteed. He signed for the London club in October 1983. He was just 17.

'Clubs really didn't care that much about you,' Niall says of his early years as a teenager at Arsenal. 'Once you got in during the morning and you did your duties and you did your training and you showered and you looked after the kit, then sometimes from two o'clock in the afternoon you were free. The club didn't really bother with you. They had promised your parents they would educate you. They had A-levels coming out of every part of me at the time I had signed. My mother fell for the whole lot. But when you get there it's more a case of: "OK, all the lads are going to a snooker hall. I'll look terrible if I don't go to the snooker hall and the bookies and all the rest of it."

'I was very lucky. I always had two sets of friends. I had the lads that I played football with every day. But although it was my 17th birthday when I signed, I was tall for my age and I hung around with lads who were 18 or 19 in Dublin and they had just started to emigrate. I had a couple of friends, including one fellow who was over on the same flight as me whom I hung around with for a long time afterwards. So I was able to go from one to the other quite easily.

I'd have the football lads, who'd be doing their thing and we'd have some kind of *craic* there. But then I'd go off to my Irish friends in another side of London. There was always something for me to do.

'The only time I ever got homesick was about three or four years later when I'd made my breakthrough. I had got on the team and played for 18 months. Then, suddenly, Alan Smith came and I wasn't getting a game and I wasn't even playing in the reserves because I was travelling with the first team and they used to play at the same time. I wasn't even on the bench and it was horrible. It was just training all week for nothing. I hadn't been involved for about a month. A couple of days before Christmas, George Graham put me in the squad of 18. I hadn't a hope of getting on the bench. I got the hump and I threw a sickie and I got a lift to Holyhead and got the boat from Holyhead and had a bit of a night out in Dublin.

'I ended up in Belvedere rugby club and came home and knocked on my mother's door and she nearly died. "What are you doing here?" she asked. I told her what had happened. The next day was Christmas Eve and I couldn't get a flight. The game they played on St Stephen's Day was live on RTÉ so I was able to see it. I got back to London that night and the next day I went into training and George Graham pulled me and said: "Where were you?" I told him I had watched the game over in the far stand with some mates, that I had the flu and I didn't want to give it to the lads. He fell for it. I got away with it. That was the only real time I pushed the boat out and probably reacted the wrong way.'

In the 1985–86 season Niall Quinn made his début for Arsenal against Liverpool, scoring in his very first game. Apart from the goal, he also set up Charlie Nicholas for another Arsenal score. Those were reasonably successful years at Highbury with the team winning the League Cup in 1987 and the League title in 1989. Although Niall hadn't accumulated enough games to win a Championship medal, he did share in the League Cup success. He also was regarded as a valuable squad member, at least until his final years when he effectively dropped out of the reckoning.

Niall also attracted the attention of the Republic of Ireland manager Jack Charlton, who selected him for his first international appearance against Iceland in May 1986. Coming on with just minutes to go in that game, he became something of a super-sub throughout the next few years. Although struggling to displace Frank Stapleton or Tony Cascarino in the Irish attack, he became a regular squad member with a series of walk-on parts in the national side. Even in his dark days at Arsenal in the late 1980s, Niall's international career brought some light into his life.

'I was a Jack Charlton babe,' Niall remarks. 'He stood by me miraculously at times because I wasn't even getting a game with the Arsenal reserves and yet I was playing international matches. My name was included every time. He never dropped me from the squad. It was incredible really. It was a lifeline for me because I wasn't playing at Arsenal but I was still getting involved with Ireland and I was still coming on as sub in the qualifiers and what have you.

'He had a great way of picking you up and making you feel great. But then, just when he felt you might be getting above yourself, he'd knock you straight back down again. I can remember turning up for one of the games at the Airport Hotel in Dublin and Jack had a kind of a press conference going on. I can remember coming in and there was a crowd of journalists standing around him. He was talking to the journalists. Maurice Setters, his assistant, was sitting down a couple of yards away. I walked in and he looked out over the top of his glasses at me and I went: "All right, Jack!" He turned and looked at Maurice and said: "Maurice, we haven't picked that big galoot?" And Maurice went: "Yes, we've picked him." And he went: "Ah, dear God almighty, we are struggling." This was in front of all the press lads. I went into that hotel feeling 8 ft tall and suddenly my shoulders dropped and I was back down again. That was his way. He probably felt that I was getting a little bit cocky at the time.

'The other thing I used to do then was when I'd get on I'd run around like a headless chicken. I was so eager to impress him. I was scared stiff about doing things wrong and I'd get all worked up and used to waste all my energy. It used to drive him mad. But eventually, as I got a little bit of experience and made the breakthrough and started for him, I learnt the way he wanted to play and it was thoroughly enjoyable. He believed in me. I was at a club where the manager didn't believe in me. I became a big part of Jack's plans and it was like a happy family. I was playing a prominent role as opposed to being the kid that was just happy to be there.'

Up to the Republic of Ireland's World Cup expedition in 1990,

Niall Quinn scored just one goal for the national side. That small tally is explained by his many appearances as sub and his limited number of caps due to competition from Stapleton, Cascarino and Aldridge. On the way to Italy, however, Niall scored again, this time in a friendly against Malta. It was to be a highly significant goal in more ways than one. Although in that match Frank Stapleton scored his record 20th goal for his country, it would be his last game in an Irish shirt. Just as importantly, Niall Quinn would soon replace him in the national side. However, it took one great performance and an equally great goal in the match against Holland in Palermo to secure that automatic slot in the team.

'It was typical of Jack,' Niall says of his late selection for the match against Holland. 'We got on the bus, went to the stadium and walked out onto the pitch. Nobody had said anything to me and I thought: "Well, that's a sure sign, Jack would have told me by now if I was playing." I was walking back in and he just said: "You know what I'm looking for from you, don't you?" I kind of said to him: "Am I playing?" He went: "Has nobody told you that you're playing?" He blamed Maurice Setters for not telling me that I was playing. Maybe it was his idea to keep me from being nervous because I didn't know until literally 45 minutes before the game that I was playing.

'We played Holland and the names just roll off the tongue: Van Basten, Gullit and other great players. But Van Breukelen is the one I remember most because he should have made a comfortable save from a long kick-out that one of his defenders played back to him. I ran in on the off-chance that he might fumble. He did and I put it away. A whole new world opened up for me. I was suddenly an international player. From that moment on, every time I was fit, until 11 years later, I started for Ireland in competitive games. It was to give me 11 years of uninterrupted play, other than injury. It was just an amazing night.'

In March 1990 Niall Quinn joined Manchester City where he quickly established himself as a favourite with the fans. In his first full season, 1990–91, he scored 20 League goals for the Manchester club. After scoring 12 League goals the following season, he subsequently suffered a cruciate ligament injury, which kept him out of the 1994 World Cup finals. He moved to Sunderland in 1996. Once more he hammered in the goals and established a lethal partnership with Kevin Phillips. More career-threatening injuries followed, although he returned to play a crucial role in the restoration of Sunderland to football prominence. Scoring as many goals as ever, Niall proved that even in their 30s players can survive the rigours of top-class football.

'I did my cruciate at Manchester City, when I really was flying,' Niall recalls. 'I was playing the best football I could. It hit me badly because in those days it wasn't as straightforward as it is now. A lot of people thought I was finished. I think if you ask Brian Horton, who was our manager at the time, he probably felt that I was never going to come back and be the player that I was. It was hard work. Then I went up to Sunderland and I did the other leg. It was hard enough but Peter Reid gave me the backing at Sunderland that I probably didn't have at City. And when Peter gave me that backing I felt I always was going to come back. He stood by me even though I went right to the edge of not making it. Millions of others wouldn't. In fact, probably nobody else would have. But I turned it around.'

Throughout the 1990s Niall Quinn steadily notched up goals for the Republic of Ireland, gradually inching closer to the record established by Frank Stapleton in 1990. He scored against Turkey, Wales, USA, Northern Ireland, Denmark, Liechtenstein and Croatia, amongst others. He also scored a crucial goal against England in the European Championship drawn match at Wembley Stadium in 1991. Having equalled Stapleton's tally in 2000, it seemed in the following 16 months that the player was suffering from either a massive mental block or sheer bad luck as he sought the elusive extra strike that would secure a new record. The vital score came, of course, in October 2001 against Cyprus. When added to his goal-scoring feats at Arsenal, Manchester City and Sunderland, Niall Quinn had established himself as one of the deadliest strikers in Irish football history.

'I never considered myself a goal-scorer,' Niall says. 'I played a type of game, especially when I first got on the team with Arsenal and things started to go well for me, where I seemed to be the foil for smaller lads. My job was to take the pressure off them and to get people into good positions and to link up with people. I would say that probably the best player at that was Teddy Sheringham and he rolled in with his share of goals over the years. I had one or two good years. I scored 20 League goals one season for Manchester City and when we went to the First Division I found it very easy with Sunderland.

'When you come to the big time, when you're playing against the best, my goal record isn't very good. But the ratio of laying on goals for other people has always been OK. You'd have to ask Ian Rush and John Aldridge and Kevin Phillips about the art of goal-scoring. They live and breathe seeing the ball hitting the back of the net. My game has always been about linking up and taking pressure off other players and using my strengths. My strengths were what got me playing until I was 35. If I had just waited around and didn't show for the ball as much as I did and waited for chances, I wouldn't have lasted as long. So I'm not jealous of other guys. My career worked out fine and somehow, amongst all that, I became the Irish goal-scoring record holder. There's a little bit of irony there somewhere.'

In 2002 Sunderland awarded Niall Quinn a testimonial as a reward for his contribution to the game. In a rare and magnanimous gesture, he donated the proceeds of the match to charities in Dublin, Sunderland and elsewhere. Contrary to the age-old football tradition of boosting a player's pension fund and providing a nest egg for rainy days, Niall's big money-spinner was a welcome windfall for the charities he chose as recipients.

Fittingly, the player was honoured in 2003 with many accolades and awards, among them an honorary MBE for his outstanding services to international football and his contribution to British charities. By then, however, he had retired after quitting football in late 2002, leaving behind memories of a prolific goal-scoring career at Arsenal, Manchester City and Sunderland. He also left in his wake his 21-goal record achieved in 91 international games.

'I would say the GAA grounding that I had was a huge plus and of huge standing to me,' Niall reflects when assessing his long career. 'Nowadays, especially with coaching and everything else, the kind of soccer player who comes to a football club at 16 years of age feels he's a real soccer player because he has been coached professionally for probably two to three years. He has been linked with big clubs. He has three or four years of people telling him he's going to be a footballer. His parents have been built up for three or four years.

'In contrast, my mother and father were shocked that I was going away to London for a week. They were disappointed that I was missing out on school. So there was none of that big build-up that you hear about and therefore the pressure wasn't on. I wasn't going to be a failure if I didn't make it. That, combined with the fact that we were predominantly a GAA family, made a big difference. There's a heart that's in GAA that's missing in professional soccer. There's something in professional sport that when it's bought it's over and done with. It's sad.

'I don't know what the correct description is of that beautiful, sparkling thing that is there in Gaelic football and hurling at the moment. The lads may as well be professional in terms of their attitude and their dedication. But when money comes into it, it's a different ball game. I don't know if the issue is cynicism or whether it's just sheer professionalism. I always try to sit on the fence when they talk about players being paid. But I'd hate to see Gaelic footballers and hurlers turn out like some of the soccer players have.

'The car I drive and the house I live in obviously demonstrate that football has been good to me. Soccer has been very rewarding to me financially. I could never knock it because of that. But if purely on a sporting basis you asked me would I rather have won a League medal with Sunderland, who paid me all this money each week, or would I swap it all for maybe one Munster hurling final with Tipperary or one All-Ireland football final with Dublin against Kerry years ago, I'd take the Gaelic football or the hurling every time.'

19. ROY KEANE

YOU WOULD BE HARD-PRESSED TO THINK OF A PLAYER AS DRIVEN AS ROY KEANE.
Words like 'intense', 'passionate' and 'committed' describe the man.
His focus and single-mindedness border on obsession. To critics he
is a flawed genius, engulfed in a world of reckless tackles, red cards
and heated controversy. To admirers he is a God-like figure, above
mere mortals, pursuing excellence, never accepting second-best.
Psychoanalysis apart, the truth is that Irish football has never seen
anyone quite like this Cork-born star.

Few Irish players have achieved more on the field of play than Roy
Keane. He has captained one of the world's greatest clubs through
one of its finest eras. He has driven his team-mates to
Championships, Doubles, a famous Treble, FA Cups and, in
particular, propelled them to European success. Few of his
contemporaries had the inner strength to return as he did from a
career-threatening injury. Fewer still had the talent to win the respect
of managers like Brian Clough and Alex Ferguson, while attracting
the interest of clubs like Juventus and Bayern Munich. Whatever his
genetic code, it ought to be copied and kept.

'I'd say a lot of it might be fear, fear of failure, and not getting carried
away with success,' Roy says of his fierce determination. 'That's just
part of my character. You look at any person who reaches the top in
sport or business and they've all got a great desire. Football's a cruel
game. I got the captaincy and two months later I snapped my cruciate
and I was out for a year. That's the way football can go. You can think:
"I've got the captaincy of Man United now, everything's going to be
great." Then I was out for a year with a snapped cruciate. So I think in
football you can never get carried away.

'I've also had very little time for people taking things for granted and who go through the motions. I've seen examples of that. I have very little time for people who maybe waste the opportunity. I think the important thing for me, when I came to England, was that I thought: "I can't really afford to be messing around because there's been a lot better players than me, with talent, who've not made it." I realised that I'm one of the lucky ones.

'I'd seen examples of players coming to England and going back to Ireland where they really blew their chance. But when I came over to England I thought: "I don't want to go to Forest for one year and go back to Ireland the following year." I thought: "I'm coming over here and I'm going to have a very good career." So when I see players messing around and throwing it away, and not making the most of the opportunity, it does irritate me. I suppose I've done it where I have messed around and I'm just grateful that I still have an opportunity to try and prove myself.

'A lot of it as well is that the people I know, they've not let me get carried away. When I was younger I probably made one or two mistakes, like every other youngster. But I have my family behind me in the last few years, my wife Theresa and my children. When you get married and have kids they give you a bit of stability. No matter how well you think you've played you go home and the kids are looking at you and they really couldn't care less how you played. They want to be entertained. So that's been a good leveller for me as well, I suppose.

'I think I'm a critical person, on myself and on the people I work with. I think I can be a demanding person. But having said that I also like to think that I'm a good team-mate to have. The way I look at the career I've got, the team has to come first. I've got no time for people who put themselves ahead of the team. Unfortunately that happens in football and people get carried away and they think they're more important than the rest of the team. So, yeah, I can be critical and I can be demanding, but that's of myself as well as of my team-mates. But I think the bottom line is that I'm a good team-mate and I'm a good team player as well.'

The Roy Keane story began at that famous Cork football academy, Rockmount, at the turn of the 1980s. Joining the club seemed a natural step as his brothers and uncles played there before him. Settling in quickly, as a nine-year-old he lined out for the U-11s. By the end of his first season he was voted Player of the Year. Those were heady days for this youngster from Mayfield, training, playing, winning trophies and medals, while watching *Match of the Day* and following Spurs. School took the back seat. Sport was the main concern.

'Like most kids, when I was growing up I was doing all sorts of sports,' Roy recalls. 'I was obviously into the GAA, I did a bit of boxing, but soccer was always my first love. The highlight of your week, when you're younger, would be watching *Match of the Day* on a Saturday night. It was always my dream to get to England to become a professional and make my mark on the game. That's what you dream of. When I go back to Ireland, kids are always asking: "Did you always want to be a footballer?" You've got to have dreams because they can come true.

'When I was at Rockmount there were people at the club I looked up to, like the people who looked after me. I was fortunate regarding the managers there and the lads I played with, who were all great lads. Regarding my heroes in England, the players I would have looked up to were Bryan Robson and Glenn Hoddle, for different reasons. I admired Bryan Robson for his attitude, his will-to-win, his courage and I liked Glenn Hoddle because technically he was an outstanding player. I had a soft spot for Spurs at the time and he was doing very well for Spurs. So I suppose those two players would have to be players I admired.'

The truth is that Cork soccer was on its knees throughout Roy Keane's formative years. The glory days of Cork Hibs and Cork Celtic had long disappeared. Cork clubs failed to secure a single League of Ireland title, Premier League or FAI Cup trophy throughout the whole of the 1980s. There had been one development of note. In 1985–86 a second-tier division had been launched as an adjunct to the new Premier League. One of the First Division's founding-members was Cobh Ramblers. It was there, at Cobh Ramblers, that Roy Keane would test his mettle with the hard men of football as the 1980s came to a close.

'It's a tough place and physically very demanding,' Roy says of the First Division. 'You've got a lot of experience in that League and if you start messing around too much they'll put you in the stand. But at that time it was right for me. I had nine years at Rockmount and you could say I needed toughening up a little bit. And, of course, I wanted to get a trial in England. So going to Cobh was a great stepping-stone for me. I had a great time at Cobh. The First Division is a learning curve and you had to be about your wits because in two minutes flat you'd have a broken leg.'

In February 1990 Roy Keane was spotted playing for Cobh Ramblers youths in a match against Belvedere Boys. He produced a towering performance that day. Having caught the attention of a scout who attended the Fairview Park encounter, he was soon on his way to Nottingham Forest on trial. Once again, he turned in a massive performance. It was enough to impress Forest's charismatic manager Brian Clough, who offered him a contract. With the deal done and dusted, Roy Keane traded Cork for Nottingham in the summer of 1990.

'I was wet behind the ears,' Roy comments on his early years with Nottingham Forest. 'You'd miss your family and your friends. And I certainly missed Cork. I look back now and think: "Bloody hell, at 18 I should have been a bit more mature." You see the young lads now and they're all very mature. But any time I went to see Brian Clough about going home, no problem. It wasn't a case of going home for two days and wanting me back on Monday. He'd always say: "Go home and come back next Thursday or Friday." He'd say that even though we'd have a game on the following Saturday. I was fortunate that the manager understood my situation.

'There were outstanding players at Forest like Des Walker, Stuart Pearce, who I've got great respect for, and Nigel Clough. It was a dream come true. From being younger watching football on *Match of the Day* on a Saturday night and then to be playing on the same pitch as some of these players, it was just fantastic for me. I think I was in the right place at the right time. I was basically thrown in the first team and I was very, very lucky. Even when I came over to Forest for my first trial, the trial happened to go well. On another day I could have played badly. I would have gone back to Cobh and that could have been the end of it. But fortunately I went to the right club at the right time. That's what you dream of.'

The rise of Roy Keane at Nottingham Forest was nothing short of dramatic. He played in the 1991 FA Cup final against Spurs. He appeared in the 1992 League Cup final against Manchester United. Although Forest lost both finals, Roy's standing in the game grew rapidly. Things didn't look quite so bright in 1993 when the club was relegated. By then, however, Roy's career was about to move in a different direction. Long admired by Manchester United manager Alex Ferguson, he was signed by the Reds in the summer of 1993.

'It was just built for success,' Roy says of the Manchester United set-up he joined in July 1993. 'I was coming into a winning team that just won the Championship the year before. I knew the foundations were right and there were a lot of good young players coming through. There was a lot of experience like Bryan Robson, Cantona, Ince, Bruce, Kanchelskis. Yet there was a lot of youth coming through like Lee Sharpe and Ryan Giggs. It was the right team for me and I knew that I could make my mark.

'Then there's the hunger the manager showed from the top. When I was leaving Forest I could have maybe gone to one or two other clubs and I was very close to going to Blackburn. But as soon as I met the manager at his house, spoke about his intentions for the team not just for that season but for the next few years, and what I could bring to the team, then that was it. As soon as I came to work with him on a day-to-day basis, I realised what football means to him. He's a winner and he sets very high standards. With the sending-offs, one or two silly things I've done off the pitch, even throughout the World Cup in 2002, the support he gave me was very important to me. So when you go out on the pitch you just try and repay the manager with performances. I think there's probably mutual respect over the years. I respect him for what he's done for me as a person, not just on the football side but off the pitch. And hopefully he's got some sort of respect for what I've helped the team achieve.'

In little over a decade following Roy Keane's arrival at Manchester United, the domestic success achieved by the club was phenomenal. Roy made his début on 7 August 1993 in the Charity Shield against Arsenal. The Premier League was won in 1994, 1996, 1997, 1999, 2000, 2001 and 2003. The FA Cup was secured in 1994, 1996, 1999 and 2004. Roy also was elevated to the club captaincy in 1997, replacing Eric Cantona following his retirement. Accompanying the highs were some dark lows, most notably the cruciate ligament injury sustained against Leeds United at the start of the 1997–98 season. That injury kept Roy out of the game for the best part of a year. For a while, it seemed that his career might be finished.

'I believe that was a very important part of my career and my life,' Roy says of his time out injured. 'The week leading up to the Leeds match I'd been out and about and been a bit of a naughty boy, with too many late nights, and then I got frustrated in the game against Leeds and ended up really kind of injuring myself by snapping my cruciate. That year was a long time out. I had a lot of time to myself. I looked at the life I was leading, the mistakes I was making and I thought to myself: "I can't keep on making these mistakes." I'd like to think I've got some sort of common sense but I was making the same mistakes. I was, at the time, I suppose, taking my career and my life for granted. But when I thought about coming back from this cruciate injury, I thought: "I'm going to make the most of what I've got here, playing for Manchester United, the facilities regarding the weights, the dieticians, medically looking after myself better."

'That year out of the game was a major turning-point, with a lot of long hours in the gym with myself and with my head, a lot of hours in the swimming-pool, and when you're not a great swimmer that's very hard. Obviously I was at home for weekends when the team were away. Theresa was there. And you just learned a hell of a lot. Sometimes you need something bad to happen to learn from it. And I look back over my career the last few years and I think I've learned more from my downs and disappointments than from the highs. If it was all about highs then I suppose you'd never appreciate them.'

The long-awaited repeat of Manchester United's 1968 European Cup success took over 30 years to arrive. When it finally came in 1999, Roy Keane was missing. Even the player's harshest critics were moved by his suspension from the final following yellow cards secured against Inter Milan and Juventus. Having already accomplished the Double, United travelled to Barcelona for the Champions League showdown against Bayern Munich. Down 1–0 at the game's death, two miraculous goals from Sheringham and Solskjaer sealed victory for the Reds. Although delighted for his team-mates, the driving force behind so many of Manchester United's European campaigns missed out on one of the club's greatest moments.

'The priority is always the team,' Roy insists. 'The time it hurts you is when the final is on. People go on about the yellow card in the Juventus match. I have no problem with the yellow card in the Juventus match. But the yellow card that hurt me was in the Inter Milan match, in the quarter-finals. There was a bit of an argument going on with two other players, nothing to do with me, and I went over and had a few words.

The referee booked me for getting involved. Even at the time he booked me I thought: "This booking could come back to haunt me." It wasn't the Juventus one because you have to make tackles and that's what I'm paid to do. I had mis-controlled the ball and Zidane was getting away from me and going on to our defence. It was getting involved in the argument with Inter Milan, with one of their players, that annoyed me more than anything else. But that's life and you move on.

'Even the night of the semi-final I felt more disappointed for Paul Scholes. Scholesy came on and he got booked and he missed the final. As a player you can be selfish but I looked at Scholesy after the match and I felt more disappointed for him. He had only just come on as sub. At least I had played the whole match and there's more of an opportunity you're going to get booked. So my heart went out to him more so than myself.'

No controversy shook the Irish soccer world quite like Roy Keane's departure from the World Cup finals in Korea and Japan in 2002. At the time, Roy was a seasoned international of 11 years' standing. He also was captain and inspiration behind the Republic of Ireland's drive to the finals. Disillusioned with the team's facilities and preparations, he departed Saipan in a welter of allegations, counter-allegations, confusion and conflict. The event split the nation in two, with those supporting manager Mick McCarthy lined up against those in the Keane camp. In retrospect, it was a defining moment in FAI history – an event which many would say exposed once and for all the old 'sure, it will do' certainties of Irish soccer. Although he later returned to the international side, the controversy of 2002 would never be forgotten.

'I hate when people or teams don't give themselves a chance,' Roy reflects. 'Because you might have the best training-pitch and the best gear doesn't mean you're going to win anything. But I think it gives you the best chance. I just hate when you go into something and it is not quite 100 per cent right. You've got it hanging over you: "What if? What if?" Especially at international level the rewards are great. We all see when the team does well, the whole country benefits. So when people start cutting corners on stuff for senior teams or U-21s or youths, then they suffer for it. I just think things have got to be right. It doesn't guarantee you're going to win the World Cup but you give yourself the best chance. At least if you come back you say:

"Well, we gave it a good go and it just wasn't to be." Whereas if you come back saying: "Was the preparation right?" and hand on heart you know that it wasn't, that's the biggest crime.

'I'm a great believer that what happens, happens. I talked about snapping my cruciate earlier and I think these things happen for a reason. I look back now on Saipan and even my first few days when we got there and the training kit doesn't arrive and the medical stuff doesn't arrive and some people might have a laugh and a joke about it or whatever. But I don't, because we're talking about the World Cup here. It wasn't the right environment for me to be there. It certainly wasn't, because I need to be working with people who want to give themselves the best chance. That wasn't the case. And again, this is 11 or 12 years of frustration, probably longer because you're looking at the youth football I had as well and the U-21s. But at senior level all my frustrations came to a head in Saipan. I look back now and it wasn't right for me to be there.

'People talk about the World Cup. Forget about the World Cup. I was quite happy to be back with my family, even though we all suffered, especially my family back in Ireland, my wife and kids. But I just felt, especially as captain, that we were conning everyone, conning the Irish fans. Of course we all know the media were on board with Mick and all this carry-on. But I just felt we were conning everyone and I didn't want to be part of it. Obviously there was disappointment with certain players' comments and whatever. But that's life and you can't keep going on in life saying: "Oh, if he said that and she said that and they did that to me." You move on and I think the team has certainly moved on.

'It was a combination of lots of things that came to a head and it was unfortunately on the eve of the World Cup. I said at the time I still would have played in the World Cup if I hadn't been accused of faking injury, which is the biggest insult to me because that's been a downside to my career where I have played when I shouldn't have played. But life goes on.'

There was a defining moment in the Republic of Ireland's World Cup qualifier with Holland in September 2001 that summarised the magnificence of Roy Keane. Wave upon wave of Dutch attacks were raining down on the Irish goal. The defence was in tatters. Confusion was rampant. Yet there, in the heart of the penalty-area, stood Roy

Keane, ball at his feet, surrounded by opponents, calmly looking about, assessing the options. Composed and assured, he dribbled the ball into the Dutch half, chewing up the seconds, running the clock down for a memorable victory. Not for the first time, he was voted Man of the Match.

That Roy Keane stood out among his peers is without dispute. As a player, he was always fiercely competitive, combining tireless running with great skill. Like all great footballers, he always had plenty of time and space. As a midfielder, he developed into a colossus. Whether building attacks or disrupting opponents, he was without compare. As a captain, he inspired and led by example. That he was the driving force behind Manchester United's great successes of the 1990s and into the 2000s no one can question. Finally, as skipper, he continued the distinguished tradition of successful Irish captaincies at Old Trafford stretching back through those great players and subsequent managers, Noel Cantwell and Jackie Carey.

'I'm very fortunate over the last few years, especially as you get a bit older you start realising there's more to life than football,' Roy concludes. 'I've got a fairly good balance in my life. Don't get me wrong, when I'm working I'm working. When I go out on that pitch I want to win and it means everything when you're out there. But if I was to retire in a year or two, the management thing is in the back of my head. It's something I'm looking at, put it that way. Maybe it's a nice challenge. You need challenges in life. I don't think you can just retire and play golf for the next 40 or 50 years. So it's something I'm looking at. I'm getting things in place for if I do want to go into it. But we'll wait and see.

'It all depends, if I did retire in a year or two, what opportunities came up for me. It would have to be the right club and I think a lot of players when they retire now are so desperate for a manager's job they'd jump into anything. I think it's important that you go and learn the trade. I think it's impossible for a player to come straight in and try and manage a big, massive club like Manchester United. People on the outside do not realise the demands that are placed on managers, especially at a big club. So I think you would have to go down a little bit and probably do your apprenticeship.

'I'm fortunate. I'm in a position where I can relax and wait for the right opportunity. I read about Kevin Keegan and when he retired he was out of football for over seven years. He spent time with his family, recharged the batteries and felt it was the right time to come back when Newcastle came calling for him. So life without football doesn't frighten me. When you're in football it's 24-hours-a-day in the demands. I think I'm more than capable of saying: "Nah, I'll look at another challenge in life." But I do think football is in my blood and it might be hard to get away from that.

'I can look back and think I'm just one of the luckiest people in the world. I don't say that lightly. It was great, no regrets. There were ups and downs. The ups always make up for the downs. I've just been very, very fortunate and there have been good people around me to look after me. It's not over yet, you know, there's plenty of challenges ahead.'

20. DAMIEN DUFF

HIS STORY CLASSICALLY ILLUSTRATES JACK CHARLTON'S LEGACY TO IRISH SOCCER. HE WAS aged nine when the Republic of Ireland played in its first major tournament, Euro '88. Like virtually all other kids at the time, he was mad into soccer. Then came Italia '90. There was a penalty shootout, a dramatic battle with Italy, glorious memories from Cagliari, Palermo, Genoa and Rome. As part of Jack's 'home' army he watched the games on television, dressed in green and white, replicating in schoolboy matches the skills of his Irish heroes.

Those were heady days in Irish soccer, when seeds were sown for a future generation of football stars. Inspired by the magic of players like Aldridge, Sheedy, Cascarino, Moran and McGrath, the budding stars grew up knowing only success, oblivious to the failures of previous generations. By the mid-1990s they began to come of age. As they appeared on the scene none surpassed the magical talents of Dubliner Damien Duff. He would in time transfer from Blackburn Rovers to Chelsea for £17 million while becoming the new kid on the block and the most exciting talent in the Republic of Ireland team.

'I think they caught everyone's imagination really,' Damien remarks of Jack Charlton's star-filled teams. 'To me all the players were legends. I remember watching all the games and wearing the jerseys. I think we watched most of the games down in the Glenside pub with my dad, having a Coke with a Guinness head. There were songs with verses about each of the players. They were brilliant, each player for different reasons.

'There was Kevin Sheedy's goal against England. Paul McGrath was always a class act along with the two big fellows up front. It was a great buzz when I came into the squad to have a chance of playing with them, players like Cascarino, Staunton and what have you. I could go on all day about them. They were great days.

'I was mad into football at the time. I started out with Leicester Celtic when I was about nine. Obviously the first step was to go join a club and I just went down and joined them. I gave up football for a while to play rugby for my school because they were rugby-orientated and they didn't really like football. Then I went to Lourdes Celtic and I finished up with St Kevin's.'

Throughout soccer history, Ireland has fed Britain with the finest of export talent. From Jackie Carey and Con Martin through Noel Cantwell and Johnny Giles up to Paul McGrath and Roy Keane, some extraordinary players have crossed the Irish Sea to play with British clubs. In the 1990s that trend continued. A new wave of youngsters who grew up through Jack Charlton's years travelled overseas in search of fame and fortune. From Tallaght came Robbie Keane. From Ballyboden came Damien Duff.

Spotted by Bray Wanderers' manager and Blackburn Rovers' Irish representative Pat Devlin, the young Damien Duff stood out among his peers. He was already testing his skills in schoolboy soccer with Leicester Celtic, Lourdes Celtic and St Kevin's Boys. Even from his early teens he showed devastating potential. 'I saw him first at the age of 13,' Pat Devlin remarks. 'He was a wisp of a fellow. You'd think he couldn't run five yards. But he had this uncanny ability to beat people and whip in crosses. He had this maturity about him that stood out. He oozed with confidence and he had a burst of pace that was incredible. He was one of the few that we felt really would make it.' With attributes like that, a move cross-channel was virtually guaranteed.

'At about 13 or 14 you start getting noticed,' Damien says. 'There are lots of scouts at schoolboy games and you'd spot them a mile off on the sidelines with their long jackets. All the young kids are trying to impress. Pat Devlin came and saw me at a game. He asked me did I want to go over and it went from there. The only other club I went to was Huddersfield and I actually wanted to sign for them. But Pat persuaded me in the end and he got me to sign for Blackburn.

'Joining Blackburn was a great buzz. It was new to me. Kenny Dalglish was still there. Working with him every day was a dream come true. I suppose it wasn't really until the second year that homesickness set in. There was a good few Irish lads there at the time. All the rest, the English and the Scots, would get to go home every weekend and we'd be left in the digs on our own. Those were really hard times.

'It didn't get to me until the second year and that's when I wanted to go home. But the club and the youth-team manager Alan Irvine were brilliant. I went in on one occasion and saw Alan Irvine and I was just crying in front of him, a big cry-baby. Ray Harford, the manager, came in as well. They were brilliant with me. They thought the best thing for me to do was not to go home because that would make it worse. So they brought my family over and looked after me.'

By the time Damien Duff arrived at Blackburn Rovers, the club were back in top-class soccer. Under the managerial guidance of Kenny Dalglish they had secured promotion to become inaugural members of the new Premier League. Great players had arrived including Alan Shearer and Chris Sutton. The Premiership was won in 1995. It seemed the great days of Blackburn Rovers were back with a vengeance. It was enough to impress any fledgling player, not least this youngster from Dublin they called 'Duffer'. 'My youth-team manager Alan Irvine was Scottish,' Damien explains regarding the nickname. 'I think the Scots throw an "er" at the end of names. So he started it and I think everyone in football, even my family, call me it now.'

From the beginning Damien demonstrated amazing skills at Ewood Park. He had consummate ball control, could feint both left and right and was capable of quick changes of direction. A natural dribbler, he possessed the sort of speed, balance and ball wizardry known only to players like Ryan Giggs in recent times and George Best and Stanley Matthews from earlier eras. He was a defender's nightmare. Whether flying down the wing or cutting inside, few young players could set pulses racing quite like Damien Duff.

Luckily, Damien arrived at Blackburn Rovers at a time when the club was expanding its youth policy. Under owner Jack Walker a youth academy was developed to foster young talent. At the Lancashire club the youth team mattered. Soon, however, Damien was making his first-team début. The opponents were Leicester City. The date was 11 May 1997. The result was an unfortunate 4–2 home defeat. Aged 18, he was voted Man of the Match.

'I was at home on my summer holidays,' Damien recalls. 'We

were struggling all year against relegation and Tony Parkes was the caretaker manager at the time. He gave me a call and said: "Come over, you're involved at the weekend." He didn't say I was playing. So he just brought myself and my ma and my da back over to England and he didn't tell me until about an hour before the game.

'It was a nice way really because it didn't give me any time to worry. I got a great night's sleep the night before, thinking I wouldn't be involved. It was a great day. We lost 4–2 but it was great for the fans because we were still in the Premiership. I got Man of the Match as well. So it was nice.'

In the summer of 1997 Damien Duff was selected for the Republic of Ireland's U-20 World Cup squad and he travelled to Malaysia for the U-20 World Youth Championship finals. It was a productive trip for Damien, who performed with distinction while helping his team secure bronze in the tournament. The game against Morocco was historic. In extra-time Damien scored the first-ever golden goal in a World Cup match at any level. The tournament launched him on the international stage and helped secure his place in the Blackburn Rovers first team for the following season.

'About four weeks after my club début I was at the U-20 World Cup,' Damien remarks. 'Brian Kerr had obviously seen something in me at the time because I was only 18. I was the only one out of my age group, I think, that went. He gave me a big boost by picking me for the squad because I was surrounded by lads two and three years older than me. We went there and we came third in the world and it is probably one of the greatest experiences of my life. It gave me a taste for big-time football. Roy Hodgson was the new manager at Blackburn and he'd obviously seen my performances over there. So he threw me in straight away that season.'

In March 1998 Damien Duff won his first senior international cap in an away game against the Czech Republic. Although the Republic of Ireland lost, Duff played well and showed many skilful touches against the Czech defence. That match was important for providing Damien, Robbie Keane and Mark Kinsella with their first senior international outings. As preparation for the imminent European Championship the exercise couldn't have been better. At least three new players came to the fore and a core of new talent was identified for the years ahead.

'It was a very proud moment,' Damien says of his first senior cap. 'Mick McCarthy brought a lot of young lads into that squad, myself and Robbie included. I think he gave out about six new caps so it was exciting. Being my first cap it was probably the proudest moment in my football career. Although we lost, it's always nice to get your first cap. But I wouldn't say my performances with Ireland really got to the level that I had expected them to be at until later.'

Throughout subsequent international campaigns, debate arose over the best role for Damien Duff in the Republic of Ireland team. Although devastating on the left wing, he was frequently chosen in an inside role as striker. Mick McCarthy's tactic was in part influenced by Duff's ability to score goals and his remarkable skill, which allowed him to play in almost any attacking position. It also was influenced by positional restrictions in the team dictated by the limited talent available. Either way, Duff's arrival in the side brought a ray of sunshine to Irish soccer.

Over time, Damien's performances improved dramatically, with an extraordinary confidence, exuberance and vitality gradually entering his game. He delivered great displays in many matches including the crucial World Cup qualifier against Holland and the pre-World Cup friendly against Denmark. His skills mesmerised the Dutch defence in September 2001. Skipping past tackles and repeatedly winning frees, his role in unsettling the Dutch was crucial in securing his team's 1–0 victory. His performance against the Danes the following March was nothing short of genius, as he single-handedly destroyed their right flank and secured one of his many Man of the Match awards in the Republic of Ireland's 3–0 victory.

'The Holland game everyone still talks about,' Damien remarks. 'It was probably the greatest day at Lansdowne Road in 10 or 20 years. There was great colour and it was a great occasion. We beat them 1–0 and some reporter thought it was hilarious and tried to have a go at me that I didn't go out celebrating that night, that I wanted to go home and watch the England game with my little brother. He made a big thing out of that. It's whatever makes you happy, isn't it? I just wanted to spend time with my family because I never get to see them. But playing for Ireland is just the proudest moment ever. Obviously your bread and butter is club football. But the biggest accolade you can get is playing for your country. It's always been the highest moment of my career.'

It took until summer 2002 and the World Cup in Korea and Japan for Damien Duff to burst onto the world stage. Having already signalled his potential in the pre-tournament game against Denmark, he travelled to Asia heavily weighed down by the burden of expectation. Despite the turmoil in the Republic of Ireland camp, no Irish player shone more brightly and few world stars emerged with their reputations as enhanced as Damien Duff's. His performances lit up the tournament, in particular his goal and his starring role in the Republic of Ireland's 3–0 defeat of Saudi Arabia. That was the match where, following his goal, Damien delivered his famous bow to the fans, which became one of the enduring images of World Cup 2002.

'I was desperate to get off the mark in the World Cup,' Damien says. 'Even though it was a jammy goal, I thought it would be good to do a nice celebration. Obviously, over there they have ways of saying hello and goodbye and I saw local people doing it. I thought it would be nice to do and it obviously caught on. I had an idea what to do earlier on in the week. But I wasn't practising it in the bathroom or anything, honest!

'I look back on the World Cup with great pleasure. It was the greatest experience of my life, playing on the biggest stage in front of the world. We came back as heroes but I don't really see it that way. I think we should have gone a lot further, especially playing against Spain with them down to 10 men for the last half-hour. We had an awful lot of chances and we should have put them away. I felt a bit guilty after Spain for not taking one of the penalties, especially after having such a good game. It was my best game in the World Cup. But I've never enjoyed taking penalties. I'm brutal at them as well. But I don't think we should have gone out at such an early stage. It was very disappointing.'

Following the World Cup, Damien Duff returned to Blackburn Rovers for the 2002–03 season. It was to be his 7th and last season at the club. He scored 9 goals in 26 Premiership games and helped Blackburn qualify for the UEFA Cup. His performances often were stunning and it was clear that he had matured into one of the most talented and explosive players in English soccer. Despite his growing fame, he continued to live on his own in the quiet Ribble Valley, far from the hustle and bustle of city life and a world removed from the glitz, glamour and hype of many footballers' lives. In the place of a frenzied lifestyle Damien, by his own admission, occupied his time by sleeping. It was once referred to by Republic of Ireland manager Brian Kerr as 'adhesive mattress syndrome' and became something of an amusing anecdote in football and media circles.

'Obviously I like my kip,' Damien asserts. 'I think a few people have gone over the top about it. But it's a hard game I work in and you need your rest. Around games I like to get a lot of sleep because I like to feel good and nice and bright and full of energy on the day of a match. I suppose that's all it really comes from. When I first came into the squad I liked to go to bed in the afternoons and have two and three hours but my mam has got me out of that. She says it's not good for me so I've left that behind now. So I suppose a couple of days a week I'd like to get a good 12-hour kip in, go to bed at around nine and get up at nine for training. I feel so good after it. But as for going to bed all day, as obviously everyone thinks I do, I used to but not any more.'

In early 2003 there was widespread speculation that Damien Duff's departure from Blackburn Rovers was imminent. Initial rumours involved Liverpool and Manchester United. Eventually, despite the player's happiness to remain at Blackburn and having signed a relatively new contract with the Lancashire club, it was Chelsea that secured his signature. Backed by Roman Abramovich's fortune, Chelsea were in the process of splashing out on Adrian Mutu from Parma, Hernan Crespo from Internazionale, Claude Makelele from Real Madrid and Juan Sebastian Veron from Manchester United. The power of money also held sway in the case of Damien Duff with Chelsea finally securing his transfer for a cool £17 million in summer 2003.

'For the last two years of my career at Blackburn I was always getting linked with the likes of Manchester United and Liverpool,' Damien recalls. 'It came as a big surprise that I went to Chelsea. But, at the end of the day, when you come down to it Chelsea were the only club bidding for me. It came down to either staying at Blackburn or going to Chelsea and it was an opportunity I couldn't turn down. They are a massive club and well on the way to becoming one of the biggest clubs in the world. It was unbelievable. I'm still a kid at heart so I was delighted going in every day and working with the likes of Desailly and Veron.

'The transfer fee was huge money and when it's changed into euros it sounds an awful lot more. But when you look at it, it's a proud thing for myself and my family. I don't really think about it until reporters mention it to me. I thought I wouldn't have handled it as well as I have done. I thought it might have got to my game at times. But it didn't, to be honest. My mam obviously holds the purse-strings. I'm not money-orientated. I'm just in it for the love of the game. I know it sounds cheesy but it's just fortunate that you get paid an awful lot of money to do what you love doing. That's the way I look at it.'

In many ways the story of Damien Duff is the story of Irish football. It's a tale of young boys who dream of playing for great teams in glorious football stadiums while winning trophies, medals and awards. Images of dark winter weekends and sunny summer days togging out for schoolboy teams characterise their early football years. They emigrate at a young age. Without their families they face loneliness, uncertainty and the prospect of catastrophic failure. For those who succeed there is the promise of riches and fame. For those who fail there's the hollow emptiness of rejection.

The route taken by Damien Duff mirrors the paths of thousands of his predecessors in the game. Early pioneers like Peter Farrell, Tommy Eglington, Con Martin and Jackie Carey were driven by the same desires. Generations of players, including Pat Jennings, Johnny Giles, Liam Brady and Frank Stapleton, took the boat to Britain. The longing to play football, to do so in the company of talented players, to prove themselves against great teams, has driven many a young Irish boy. Most have failed. Others, like Damien Duff, have struck gold while inspiring future generations of young Irish footballers to seek careers in the professional game.

'I'm just a kid that loves playing football,' Damien concludes. 'I want to be a world-class player, first and foremost. I work hard at the game and that's what I want to do. I've had a lot of breaks and that's the way it happens in football. So I'm very lucky and I appreciate everything that I get.'